What Thought Leaders Ar
The Book of Agree

"We all want agreement. Here's how to get it ...u keep it and work it."
—Mark Victor Hansen, Co-creator, *The New York Times* #1 bestselling series, *Chicken Soup for the Soul*®

"Buy this book. I know systems for creating wealth. The systems in *The Book of Agreement* will help you create the kind of agreements that will generate much more financial and emotional wealth in your life."
—Robert Allen, author of four New York Times bestsellers, *Crating Wealth, Multiple Streams of Income, Multiple Streams of Internet Income*, and the phenomenal *Nothing Down*.

"*The Book of Agreement* contains all the models you'll ever need to protect questionable relationships and nurture strong relationships. It puts some iron in the handshake."
—Alan Weiss, Ph.D., Author, *The Ultimate Consutlant*

"The day after I read Stewart Levine's *The Book of Agreement*, I was able to put his principles and prescriptions to the test. They worked for me, and I know they'll work for you! Levine's approach is so straightforward and so sound that you just can't miss. It was like a whack on the side of the head when I read Levine's simply profound and sensible notion that we'd all benefit from embracing the idea of creating agreements for results instead of negotiating agreements for protection. Putting that concept into practice in all our relationships is what this book is about, and the pages are full of very explicit advice on how to do it. My prediction is that you'll be consulting *The Book of Agreement* before engaging in any new negotiation, and you'll be very glad that you did. In fact, I bet you have one tomorrow, so what are you waiting for? Buy this book right now!"
—James M. Kouzes, Co-author, *The Leadership Challenge* and *Encouraging the Heart;* Chairman Emeritus, Tom Peters Company

"Every year, in law schools across the country, each new generation of future lawyers learns to reproduce the mistrust that is the great tragedy of our individualistic and isolating society by learning that the purpose of legal agreements, or contracts, is to protect you from the Other, that stranger at arm's length who is out to exploit you for his or her own self-interest. Stewart Levine begins from the exact opposite premise—that the purpose of agreement is to build a bridge to the Other and to realize your common aspiration for connection. Writ large, this idea would revolutionize the study and practice of law and help realize our spiritual nature as social beings in pursuit of mutual affirmation."

—Peter Gabel, Professor of Contract Law, New College Law School; Associate Editor, *Tikkun Magazine*; President of the Board, New College of California; Director, Institute for Spirituality and Politics

"A wonderful, comprehensive look at the potential for agreement in the world. Stewart describes the agreements we aspire to and tells you how to avoid the calamities you fear and how to get the results you want. This is good stuff!"

—Geoff Bellman, Consultant; Author of *Getting Things Done When You Are Not in Charge*

"Now, more than ever, we need to learn how to work toward agreement rather than let conflict tear us apart. Stewart Levine's new book is an important step in the right direction."

—B. J. Gallagher Hateley, author of *What Would Buddha Do at Work?* and *A Peacock in the Land of Penguins*

"Stewart Levine, where have you been all my life? And why did it take you so long to write *The Book of Agreement*? But now that you have—Thanks! I can't promise to reform my errant ways, but now at least I will understand how I got there and what might be done in terms of extrication. And I think all other similarly challenged individuals will find the book a godsend. Try it!"

—Harrison Owen, author of *Open Space Technology*

"Stewart Levine has managed to bring his years of considerable experience, plus his wit, charm, and clarity, to a book that will enable the reader to come to true agreement. While this book is useful to anyone, it can be especially helpful to the business leader and the world leader. Bravo!"

—Robert Fritz, author of *The Path of Least Resistance, Creating* and *The Path of Least Resistance for Managers*

"Agreements that serve everyone well help us create a cooperative civilization—one that can creatively include competition and conflict, as well as love and community, even among strangers. Stewart Levine provides some sensible tools to build that civilization together, piece by piece, as the need arises in our own lives and work."
—**Tom Atlee, Founder, The Co-Intelligence Institute**

"Most books on legal subjects are efficient, dry, and erudite. Stewart's book uses the heart to inform the mind. What results is an enduring work that teaches a commonsense process for reaching sustainable agreements in our business lives and personal relationships."
—**George Kaufman, Esq., author of *The Lawyer's Guide to Balancing Life and Work;* Vice Chair, Omega Institute; formerly of counsel, Arnold & Porter**

"This book shows us how horribly deficient our current agreement process is and how to create new agreements that result in real performance and satisfaction. Can we eliminate misunderstanding and conflict? Maybe not entirely, but this book comes as close to showing a way as ever before."
—**Peter B. Grazier, President, Teambuildinginc.com and author of *Before It's Too Late* and *Power Up for Team Results***

"Stewart's book helps readers to size up each opportunity to reach an agreement and maximizes the chances that each new agreement will culminate in mutually satisfying results. If you're trying to double the number of agreements you reach, and double the outcome from those agreements, Stewart's *Book of Agreement* is an invaluable guide."
—**Tom Brown, Editor, *Management General***

"In this wise and humane book, Stewart Levine makes it clear once and for all that our standard approaches to building agreements must change. More than that, he provides the tools—both philosophical and practical—for individuals and institutions to transform their approaches and in so doing build a better world."
—**Steven Keeva, Assistant Managing Editor, *American Bar Association Journal;* and author, *Transforming Practices: Finding Joy and Satisfaction in the Legal Life***

"Stewart's book reminds us how agreements pervade every aspect of our lives and provides the reader with a clear road map to more effective agreement making. After practicing law for 25 years, both as a trial lawyer and a general counsel, I never imagined that a book about agreements could be such a refreshing and enjoyable read! I recommend this book to all lawyers seriously interested in obtaining greater insight into and understanding of how to turn conflict into agreement."

—Shelby Rogers, COO and General Counsel, State Bar of Texas; former Chair, Law Practice Management Section, American Bar Association

"Lawyers will find this a how-to manual for practicing law in the new paradigm. Non-lawyers will find it a breath of fresh air that inspires them to put their visions on paper—not just for their business deals but alsofor every relationship in their lives! *The Book of Agreement* shows how to build a foundation of integrity in all areas of our lives and work."

—J. Kim Wright, President and founder of Renaissance Lawyer Society; President, The Conscious Coach, Inc.; Author of *Legal Toolkit for the Conscious Coach*; Principal, www.jkimwright.com

"Levine provides very useful tools for lawyers and clients who want to prevent and manage *future* conflicts by addressing *present* differences. His models will help people forming new collaborations deal more effectively with differences of perspective, and the many unknowns of a partnership, so that they can work together to create a stronger partnership, prevent hostility, and better manage conflicts that surface."

—Frederick Hertz, Esq., Attorney, mediator, Adjunct Professor, Golden Gate University School of Law; Author of *Legal Affairs* (Henry Holt, 1998)

"Stewart Levine's *The Book of Agreement* provides a useful and effective model to help us reach agreements that live up to our hopes and expectations. He has synthesized a wealth of wisdom and experience into a simple and elegant approach to agreements. The process of creating this kind of agreement can deepen relationships, strengthen commitment to goals, and nurture the spirit of cooperation and partnership. These are simple and powerful tools all children and adults should learn."

—D'Arcy Lyness, Ph.D., Child psychologist; Adjunct Professor, Saint Joseph's University; Editor, *Human Diseases and Conditions: Supplement 1: Behavioral Health* (Scribner's, 2001); Contributing Editor, KidsHealth.org

THE BOOK
OF AGREEMENT

Also by Stewart Levine
Getting to Resolution: Turning Conflict into Collaboration

We write because we have to say what we believe. We discover
what we believe because we write. All else of writing is but a searching
for form, a style, a technique, to show those beliefs in an acceptable artistic
manner. When we succeed our hearts are on the stage to touch the hearts
and minds of the audiences. It is an awesome experience.
—Unknown

THE BOOK OF AGREEMENT

10 Essential Elements for Getting the Results You Want

Stewart Levine

BERRETT-KOEHLER PUBLISHERS, INC.
San Francisco

Berrett-Koehler Publishers, Inc.
235 Montgomery Street, Suite 650
San Francisco, CA 94104-2916
Tel: (415) 288-0260   Fax: (415) 362-2512
www.bkconnection.com

ORDERING INFORMATION

Quantity sales. Special discounts are available on quantity purchases by corporations, associations, and others. For details, contact the "Special Sales Department" at the Berrett-Koehler address above.

Individual sales. Berrett-Koehler publications are available through most bookstores. They can also be ordered direct from Berrett-Koehler: Tel: (800) 929-2929; Fax: (802) 864-7626; www.bkconnection.com

Orders for college textbook/course adoption use. Please contact Berrett-Koehler: Tel: (800) 929-2929; Fax: (802) 864-7626.

Orders by U.S. trade bookstores and wholesalers. Please contact Publishers Group West, 1700 Fourth Street, Berkeley, CA 94710. Tel: (510) 528-1444; Fax (510) 528-3444.

Berrett-Koehler and the BK logo are registered trademarks of Berrett-Koehler Publishers, Inc.

Printed in the United States of America

Berrett-Koehler books are printed on long-lasting acid-free paper. When it is available, we choose paper that has been manufactured by environmentally responsible processes. These may include using trees grown in sustainable forests, incorporating recycled paper, minimizing chlorine in bleaching, or recycling the energy produced at the paper mill.

Library of Congress Cataloging-in-Publication Data
Levine, Stewart.
  The book of agreement : 10 essential elements for getting the results you want / Stewart Levine.
      p. cm.
  Includes bibliographical references and index.
  ISBN 1-57675-179-1
  1. Negotiation.   2. Conflict management.   I. Title.
  BF637.N4 L45 2002
  302.3—dc21   2002026006

FIRST EDITION
07 06 05 04 03 02   10 9 8 7 6 5 4 3 2 1

Designed by Detta Penna

Copyedited by Judy Johnstone

Proofread by Linda Ward

Indexed by Joan Dickey

For Marty and Janet

and

Ethel and Irving

and

all who receive abundance

because of what they give

A human being is part of the whole called by us "Universe," a part limited in time and space. He experiences himself, his thoughts and feelings as some-thing separated from the rest, a kind of optical delusion of consciousness. This delusion is a kind of prison for us, restricting us to our personal desires and to affection for a few persons near us. Our task must be to free ourselves from this prison by widening our circle of compassion to embrace all living creatures and the whole of nature in its beauty.
—Albert Einstein

CONTENTS

• • • • • • • •

PART III
PROFESSIONAL AND BUSINESS RELATIONSHIPS
141

PART IV
PERSONAL APPLICATIONS
177

PART V
CREATING A CULTURE OF AGREEMENT AND RESOLUTION
211

FOREWORD

• • • • • • • •

Why is this book so needed?

As a former freelance legal secretary/paralegal who worked for more than five hundred lawyers in every field of law between 1976 and 1995, I can recall hundreds of cases where even a little of Stewart Levine's compassionate common sense would have made a huge difference in people's lives. Upon reflection, three themes emerge.

Too many contracts are poorly drafted. A single sentence in one contract ran for three pages. Comprised of a dizzying array of "whereases" and "wherefores" that were countered by several "notwithstandings," the sentence supposedly answered two simple questions: "When does one of the parties have to pay a late fee to another party? How much?"

Most of the contracts I helped type over the years were perfect examples of what Stewart calls "fear-based" agreements. They were designed less to support whatever vision people wanted to accomplish than to limit liability should something go wrong. Because it is impossible to foresee all problems, fear-based contracts are more likely to lead to confusion (and further lawyer fees) than to create clarity and satisfaction.

Fear or misunderstanding of the contract process prevents many people from seeking the help they need to craft good agreements. A woman I'll call Mary was forced by a court to sell her home at below-market value to a tenant who was the son of her close friend. Though Mary had intended only to rent her house temporarily while she was out of the area, she had signed a contract (drawn up by a real estate agent who was a friend of her friend) that contained a very unfavorable "option to buy" clause.

"When I protested that clause," Mary later said, "I was told it was just a formality. When I thought about getting a lawyer to represent me, I remembered my father's warning that the fastest way to ruin a good friendship is to bring a lawyer to the table. I also assumed that because the agent was a friend of a trusted friend, I could trust him. By the time I realized how untrustworthy he was, I'd lost my house and my friendship."

The heart and soul of the legal system contains processes for helping people deal with their worst aspects and bring out their best. Like most people in long-term relationships, I've been tempted to walk away from my wedding vows. The temptations were most frequent during the early 1990s, when my husband John was out of work, three close relatives were dying across the country, and I was doing a lot of overtime work as a legal secretary to pay the bills. During that time, I had a vision of my current business, and I was blaming my husband for the fact that I wasn't moving toward it faster.

One day, while looking through the thick files of a contract negotiation, I was stunned by the beauty of it all. Out of these notes and letters and drafts emerged a story of two clients I'll call Joe and Janice, who were going into business together. Unlike Mary, Joe and Janice were each represented by good lawyers who helped them take off their rose-colored glasses and get clear about what was needed to make their common dreams work. Yes, Joe's lawyer was there primarily to support him, while Janice's lawyer was there to support her, but together they were committed to creating something bigger than either of them. Like the people who had stood with John and me at our wedding, the lawyers were witnesses to hope and reminders of the hard work that would be necessary to fulfill that hope.

Soon after that realization, our marriage strengthened as my attitude toward law shifted, and vice versa. I began to see that the legal work I was doing to pay the bills was not something separate from the best in our life but an essential part of it. The habits I had to develop in order to work for lawyers, like being attentive or trading assumptions for clarity, were also basic lessons for satisfying life and creative work. I began to see that contracts for such mundane things as renting a house or building a business could be as meaningful as the covenant of marriage.

Frustrated in my search for people who were interested in talking openly about such matters, I searched the Internet under the words "spirit AND law." Of the perhaps four or five names that showed up, only Stewart Levine lived nearby.

Stewart Levine in person is much like Stewart Levine the author. He has that rare gift of making me think simultaneously, "Wow! What a great new idea!" and, "Oh, yeah, everybody knows that, but why didn't anyone say it before?" Then, with his usual simply elegant style, he creates a wonderfully fertile climate that generates more new-old ideas.

Stewart's first book, *Getting to Resolution,* was brilliant. Combining legal experience with human wisdom and a sense of humor, it shows how to create an "attitude of resolution" that leads naturally to a new relationship in which the parties can heal, grow, and create a new vision for their life or work.

In *The Book of Agreement,* Stewart has distilled the best of the contracts process, stretched it, deepened it, and broadened it. I can imagine that because of this book, many artists and lovers and business people will take time to ponder such questions as "What do we want to create?" and "What do we need from each other to make that happen?"

I don't imagine that *The Book of Agreement* will make lawyers obsolete. Stewart Levine is not out to denigrate the legal system. For many years he has been in the forefront of a movement to reclaim the best of the system and to create new ways to better serve the needs of clients, lawyers, and the public at large. *The Book of Agreement* offers attorneys some much-needed guidance in crafting agreements that are simpler and truer to the needs and visions of their clients. For individuals and groups, *The Book of Agreement* offers information that sharpens our discernment skills. When do we need a lawyer's help, and when are we called to do our own work? When do we need to trust traditional wisdom, and when do we need to create new ways of crafting and fulfilling agreements? How do we know when we are well served by another and when we are not?

Because *The Book of Agreement* is a ground-breaking book, perhaps it should come with a warning: Do not read if you are determined to protect your prejudices or your limited view of the world. Stewart's thoughts will leap off the pages of this book and into your mind and heart. They will not go away. Instead, they will stir your own thinking and dreaming. You will no longer be satisfied with a world that's hampered by complicated contracts. Instead, you'll be more willing to take on the work of creating clarity based on thoughtfulness and mutual respect.

Thank you Stewart!

Pat Sullivan
Founder, Visionary Resources
Former columnist, *San Francisco Chronicle,* Business Section
Author, *Work with Meaning, Work with Joy:
How to Bring Your Spirit to Any Job*

PREFACE

• • • • • • •

I was walking down Market Street in Philadelphia when the idea of "agreements for results" first emerged. I had recently hired a highly touted guru to help me figure out my next career move. We were trying to take my experience and articulate an innovative service offering a wise, trustworthy, skillful "recovering" lawyer might provide. That was an important point on the odyssey that has been my quest for the past twenty-five years. I had been looking for the way to create cultures of agreement and resolution within all of our social institutions so that we can reduce needless and costly conflict. At that time my experience included:

- New Jersey Deputy Attorney General
- Ten years practicing law, including many civil and criminal trials
- Time with a boutique Manhattan law firm representing public corporations, doing complex real-estate transactions, and structuring then-legal tax shelter syndications
- Six years in the AT&T marketing department serving major national law firms while AT&T was going through divestiture
- A teaching fellowship at Temple University Law School
- Reflections on my personal mission and social contribution

Through my responses to a series of questions I started to see the positive vision of agreements as "road maps" and "wilderness guides" for people who were moving into unknown arenas. I kept having the vision of trusted advisors helping clients navigate major life changes and transitions using the vehicle of "agreements for results" to develop a positive vision for their future. Making this a reality has been my consuming passion. It is not easy to establish a new perspective. The dominant culture likes its way of doing things. Fortunately, when things were really rough, I could turn to the wisdom of people like Dr. Scott Peck, who reminded me that "many are called, few choose." It has been a long journey, but my voice is now part of a growing chorus.

We collaborate by forming agreements. The agreements are either expressed (spoken or written) or implied (assumed). Usually, the cause of conflict is the lack of a clear agreement. Either we did not take the time or we did not know what we needed to talk about to craft an effective, explicit agreement. It is surprising that this is a skill we were never taught, given that crafting agreements with others is a fundamental life skill. This is especially true in view of the huge cost of conflict that results from our implicit, inartful, incomplete agreements. These agreements do not effectively express a joint vision or generate a collaborative partnership. One cause of the agreement breakdown is that the process of forming the agreement is seen as negotiating in an adversarial process through which you try to win.

Because of the way we have been conditioned by our culture, for most people, negotiating an agreement is experienced as an adversarial process. Most of us have been conditioned to function in a "me versus them" context. Negotiating is a process within which you try to advantage yourself. The negotiation is not held as a process intended to express a clear joint vision, with a road map to desired results. *I believe everyone would benefit greatly if we embraced the idea of creating agreements for results and stopped negotiating agreements for protection.* The new thinking in *The Book of Agreement* is to shift the context of the process of forming agreements from an adversarial win/lose negotiating to a joint visioning process that articulates an inclusive vision of outcomes and a road map to the composite of desired results that everyone agrees on. It is a fundamental shift from the traditional idea of agreements for protection that focus on providing remedies for what goes wrong to designing agreements for results that express a joint vision that satisfies everyone. The idea is to shift our thinking from "you *or* me" to "you *and* me."

As a young lawyer, I often worked with people who had to resolve conflicts in court. They usually ended up in a courtroom because their thinking and attitude (or the thinking and attitude of their advisors) toward conflict made their situation worse. But behind that attitude is something much more fundamental. Conflicts were generated because people's agreements were incomplete or inaccurate. This revelation had greater clarity when I stopped practicing law and my work required forming new business relationships. As a business developer, with the primary goal of creating relationships, I quickly realized that most people do not know what dialogue to have that will generate a collaborative agreement.

This is true in partnerships, joint ventures, inside organizations, between organizations, and in personal relationships. It happens because we are conditioned to negotiate for protection! It's understandable. We never learned a core competence for effective living—making agreements for results that embrace others as real partners with whom we want to succeed. Instead, we have become stuck in a competitive model that says it's them or me, not them and me. This book provides that fundamental life competence that would have been very useful to learn when we were young.

As I started working with these new agreements with clients, I noticed how excited people became and how simple it was to create a new framework for any form of collaboration. The simple shift in perspective had me thinking I had invented sliced bread! As a lawyer, I had some initial concern about the "legality" of the agreements I was preparing. I quickly realized that the agreements did have legal effect, but that was not their purpose. Much more important, they provided a new lens through which to view the world as I shifted my perspective from an adversarial orientation of "how can I win by protecting my client more than you protect your client" to the idea of "how can everyone get the results they desire from this collaboration." I came to realize that although creating a meeting of the minds was very important, it was also important to create a meeting of the hearts. That is what I was doing, and that is why people were responding so favorably. Almost fifteen years of preparing agreements for results have taught me a lot about their value. I will do my best to share it with you. The following paragraph sums up our current thinking and is a core message of this book.

> **It is always important to remember that just beneath the anger of a conflict that results from a poor agreement is the sadness of a disappointed expectation. Someone anticipated and expected a specific result that did not happen. This book shows you how to minimize the conflict of disappointed expectations. Following the templates in *The Book of Agreement* enables collaborators to manage each other's expectations by making the specific purpose of the collaboration explicit.**

This book shows us how to minimize the adversarial element we may bring to the negotiation process by shifting the focus from what can go wrong, and fighting to protect against it, to a process of jointly visioning the results everyone wants to produce. The book provides tools for preventing and managing *future* conflicts by addressing *present* differences. Its models help people forming new collaborations deal more effectively with differences of perspective and the many unknowns of a partnership so that they can work together to create stronger long-term collaborations, prevent hostility, and better manage conflicts that do surface. In the process of crafting an agreement for results, people have the experience of true collaboration as they articulate needs, concerns, and fears. This leads to covenantal relationships and provides the foundation for enduring collaborations.

Acknowledgments

Special thanks to Marsha Shenk for asking the right questions. Her listening helped distill what was positive and profound from my rant against lawyers and the legal profession.

Thanks to Steve Piersanti for seeing the contribution, then promoting and coaxing what I was not quite ready to do. Kudos to the entire Berrett-Koehler staff for the many things they do, from marketing to distribution to managing the office. They are an amazing group with a noble mission. Profound thanks to the five manuscript reviewers, the designer Detta Penna, and the copyeditor Judy Johnstone. To pre-publication endorsers, I thank you for the inspiration of your thoughtful comments.

I am grateful to the clients and students who have taught me so much and provided a rich context for learning. Special thanks to those who have paid me for the privilege of working with them. To the early innovators, thank you for your special courage and pioneering spirit.

For friends, relatives, and family, who have provided counsel and comfort and have listened to my poetry, I am profoundly grateful. I thank Ethel and Irving for their love, Meyer and Adeline for their acceptance and strength. I thank Janet for dancing and Marty for her gracious presence, generous heart, and enduring friendship.

And to all of my perfect clients, colleagues, and collaborators who will be attracted by this book, I look forward to meeting and serving you.

Stewart Levine, June 2002

Revolution never depended on any one man. A strong man is acted upon by the thoughts of others. He is a sensitive plate on which impressions are made —and his vivid personality gathers up these many convictions, concentrates them into one focus, and then expresses them. The great man is the one who first expresses what the many believe. He is a voice for the voiceless, and gives in trumpet tones what others would if they could.

—Elbert Hubbard

INTRODUCTION:
WELCOME TO THE WORLD OF
AGREEMENT AND RESOLUTION

● ● ● -● ● ● ●

Some people see things as they are and say "Why."
I dream things that never were and say "Why not."
—George Bernard Shaw

Congratulations on making the choice to read this book. You are embarking on a learning process that will make you conscious of the ways relationships, productivity, and collaboration are intertwined. This book will teach you a fundamental life skill that we were never taught. Not having this skill has been very costly. Some costs you are already aware of; other costs you will realize as you read. As you use, and continue to use, the book as a reference tool, please share its ideas with others. My vision is that by sharing ideas, we can shift from a culture of distrust and separation to one of trust and connection. You will find sections with sample agreements for (1) business organizations, including all levels of management and many facets of corporate life; (2) professionals, including realtors, therapists, consultants, contractors, physicians, dentists, architects, coaches, and lawyers; and (3) personal relationships, including spouses, significant others, children, and families.

Agreements for Results

I have not seen any written material that frames effective collaboration, high levels of productivity, and personal satisfaction as a result of explicit agreements. What makes our current perspective startling is that we have been crafting agreements, and the relationships they frame, from a context of negotiation—and the way we think about negotiation is nominally collaborative but essentially adversarial. We begin negotiating as if our collaborator were our adversary! This book sets forth an operative premise that we can arrive at a joint vision of desired results from the common ground that incorporates everyone's concerns. *Working from this premise allows us to craft agreements for inclusive results based on a joint vision of outcomes* rather than worrying about what can go wrong and focusing on protection.

Agreement Continuum Characteristics

No agreement	*Legalistic agreement for protection*	*Results based on agreement*
Implicit	Explicit	Explicit
Conflict	Power	Cooperation
Chaos	Fear	Collaboration

The accompanying chart illustrates the continuum of agreements, from no agreement to a results-based agreement, and shows the different relationships that develop from the approach used. When we have no agreements, we experience a sense of chaos. Everyone, when operating from self-interest, is "doing their own thing" without a clear understanding of what others are doing, and the operative concerns motivating behavior.

I believe formal legal agreements have their origin in the hierarchy of the feudal system. It's not surprising that power and fear are infused in the process. We're using a way of thinking and processes derived from a historic context that is very different from the educated, technological world we inhabit. The same phenomenon and controlling values are embedded in the operation of our courts. That's why courthouses are generally not the place to go for justice. Isn't it time for a change?

The purpose of this book is to introduce you to the simple and powerful tools of agreements for results, whose purpose is to create collaborative partnerships. You will find templates you can use as guides for crafting your own agreements. The templates are taken from real client situations I have worked with over the past fifteen years. For privacy reasons names have been changed, and sometimes I have used composites because they are better examples. The book highlights:

- The difference between *agreements for results* and *agreements for protection*
- The *Ten Essential Elements* of *agreements for results*—what you need to fully discuss to create a covenant-based, heartfelt agreement
- Templates of *effective agreements* for organizational, professional, joint venture, and personal situations
- The *value of constructing agreements for results*
- The perspective of seeing the construction of agreements through authentic dialogue as *trust-generating success tools*

Getting to Resolution

Conflict usually arises because our agreement was inadequate. We can eliminate a great deal of conflict if we begin with a solid agreement. In *Getting to Resolution*[1] I provided the conversational Resolutionary Model[2] for resolving conflict (Chapter 6 has a good summary). The model helps you understand that the final step in resolving any conflict is putting in place a new agreement that incorporates the terms of the resolution and redefines the business or personal relationship.

When we move into action before we have built the solid foundation of an agreement for results, we often end up in conflict that has a transaction cost attached to it. I call this the *cost of conflict*. When conflict surfaces, even when you had a good agreement, you pay the transaction cost. It includes direct, productivity, opportunity, continuity, and emotional costs:

Direct—cost of professionals to help resolve

Productivity—lost time from work or diminished capacity

Opportunity—value you might be creating

Continuity—the cost of replacing valued contributors

Emotional—dampened spirit and diminished life energy

If you can develop the ability to bypass the knee-jerk reaction in evaluating a conflict situation by thinking about winning, who's right and who's wrong, who's to blame, and who needs to be punished, then you can move straight from something that's not working to creating a new agreement for results. (It's challenging to change your thinking, but have patience with yourself!) Resolving conflict could be that simple. Until that time, you can use the Resolutionary Model to get to a new agreement when conflict comes up. I say *when* because no matter how good your agreement is, some conflict will surface. Some conflict is also likely to surface in building an agreement for a new project or relationship. The Resolutionary Model is useful in either context.

Contents

Part I contains an explanation of agreements for results, along with templates and the principles on which they are based. The principles provide the logical and theoretical foundation from which the

Ten Essential Elements arise. Chapter 3 contrasts collaborative agreements for results with agreements for protection.

Part II consists of agreement "forms" for many aspects of organizational life. Given the flattened, self-directed, entrepreneurial, globalized, virtual world we live in, these agreements are becoming increasingly important.

Part III contains samples for professional and business relationships. It addresses consumers of services and their service providers. The goal is to demonstrate the value of agreements that detail anticipated results and mutual promises and, most important, that clearly manage expectations about the nature of the relationship and set forth specifics about the promised performance of the "professional." This can be especially comforting if you've never been involved with the particular kind of service before.

Just as the traditional parameters that govern organizational relationships have changed, so have those that govern personal and family relationships. It used to be that the nature of the relationship implied a set of expectations. Those implied expectations have broken down because everyone has the freedom to negotiate and articulate the unique parameters of personal relationships. Some possibilities for individuals and families are contained in Part IV.

Part V contains an implementation plan. The material of this book is not intended as an intellectual, academic experience. To understand and not use it is a waste of time. This part of the text provides a plan by which you can take control and put in place detailed agreements in all areas of your life. In *Getting to Resolution* I showed you how to get out of trouble once you're in it. This book is about staying out of trouble. More important, it's about *thriving*. It provides practical tools that can enable everyone to realize their vision through using the detail and power of agreements for results.

The book contains templates that may seem similar. That's because over the past fifteen years I was personally involved with them. As you begin working with the principles, ten elements, and samples, please stay mindful of the ways they must be modified to reflect your unique circumstances. These agreements are simple. They return us to fundamental basics we know to be true. You might say agreements for results represent a return to a "new old paradigm," the one that was in place before we all started acting like lawyers negotiating for protection. The agreements in this book reflect what we left behind as we became "sophisticated." My experience tells me we need to go back to these deeper fundamental truths. Although they are simple, they are not easy. The challenge is to make sure you have an agreement before you move forward.

Contexts

It is important to remain mindful of the context in which you are operating. Different rules, standards, and expectations are present in different situations. To have successful collaborations, we need to have awareness of the accepted operative standards and the ways in which they are changing. There was a time when, in most contexts, even without a clearly articulated agreement, widely accepted parameters provided standards and boundaries. We had sets of shared expectations about the way things were supposed to be, both in the business world and in our personal lives.

That has changed. In both business and personal situations, we are living in a world of globalization and free agency. Given a lack of universally accepted standards, every context opens the potential to craft an original articulation of what the terms are. The good news is that we have the freedom and privilege of "making it up" each time. The bad news is that with this freedom comes the responsibility to do so. And that requires focus and attention. The material in this book is simple to understand, but it is not easy to implement. We are not in the habit of taking the time to craft agreements for results, and most people don't even know what they are.

The contexts addressed in this book include business organizations, government, the nonprofit sector, and changing personal demographics.

Business Organizations

Agreements for results provide a clear path to follow and a road map to desired results. This is true for senior executives, for the employment relationship, among team members, for joint ventures with external organizations, and for projects of all kinds. Although this need has always been present, agreements for results are particularly important in the world of knowledge workers who are engaged in intellectual and creative projects for which there is no prescriptive path.

Historically, people went to work with the following mantras: (1) do what you are told; (2) don't make too much noise; (3) wait your turn and after thirty-five years retire from the same company where you started; and (4) pick up your gold watch at your good-bye dinner.

Organizations had multiple layers. The idea of a good "self-starter" was someone who did not have to be told what to do each morning. If you showed up dressed and groomed properly each day, you had a good chance of having a job for life. That was my observation of the AT&T culture when I went to work for Ma Bell in 1981. Things have changed—more than a little! We have undergone dynamic shifts in our organizational life. Over the past fifty years we have changed our predominating organizational culture and structure because of:

- The explosion of knowledge workers
- The end of the "job"
- Downsizing and rightsizing (whatever the euphemism is for layoffs)
- Reengineering
- Self-managed teams and organizations

- The flattening of organizational structures
- Technology and the Internet
- Telecommuting
- Unprecedented stock market participation
- Stock options
- The concept of free agency
- Brand "Me"
- The learning organization
- Merger mania
- Golden parachutes
- Executive MBAs
- Employment litigation
- "Projects" as an organizing principle
- Dot.com mania and its ongoing aftermath
- The workplace as primary community
- People relying on their "work family"
- The virtual organization
- Individuals as consultants or independent contractors
- The growth of contract employees
- Recession

Given an evolving workplace of knowledge workers with fewer rules and greater autonomy, people need navigation tools. In addition, the breakdown of the restrictive hierarchy and the evolution of project teams provides a need for tools that will help us create structure for each cross-functional project team of which we are a part. Along with the freedom to do it our way comes the responsibility to make sure it gets done—on budget, on time, and with the requisite amount of innovation. Crafting an agreement for results at the beginning of a project provides the structure that is essential for success.

The Government

At one time, the government was a great place to put in your time and collect a pension. This is no longer true—certainly not since the "reinvention of government" and for quite some time before that. Although not on the leading edge in the same way as for-profit business, the government has experienced significant performance pressure over the past twenty-five years. Everyone is demanding better and more sophisticated service. Given the breakdown of traditional family structure and religious institutions, more and more people look to government agencies to provide support services and a social safety net. Because of the increased demand for services, government has been adopting many of the same management innovations to improve productivity and service as the private sector. Given the introduction of performance management, the needs for tools that foster collaboration are not much different in the government from in the private sector.

The Not-for-Profit Sector

The proliferation of NGOs has been dramatic during the past few decades. Many NGOs have been formed to take up the slack on the edges of the social-assistance capacity of government. Everything has become professionalized, and the huge growth in professional associations and industry groups reflects the appetite for resources. Some of the NGOs are similar to the government when compared to the for-profits. They are just behind the leading edge in terms of management practices, but they are reorganizing rapidly so they can provide the service demanded by leading-edge professionals.

Changing Personal Demographics

The structure of our society has changed profoundly. The images of a white Protestant mom and dad with two kids; an extended family of aunts, uncles, cousins, and grandparents; and a house with a picket fence are history. We have changed, in many ways, the context in which we live. Some of these contextual changes include:

- Breakup of large, extended families due to patterns of education and mobility
- Mobility, as people make choices or are transferred by their organizations
- Changing ethnic and racial demographics (confirmed by the 2000 census)
- Breakdown of traditional religions
- The Sixties revolution, including recreational drugs and the sexual revolution
- Higher levels of college, graduate, and professional education
- Tolerance for group homes, communal living, out-of-wedlock children
- Genetic engineering, biotechnology, and the explosion of psychotropic drugs
- Increased levels of prosperity
- Embracing alternative lifestyles and redesigning the concept of family
- Globalization

As our context changed, there arose a need for dealing with all types of freedom. This means that *there is a need to articulate rules as you go along or face the conflicts uncertainty will bring.* These changes have left implicit standards in the dust. In the *negotiated* world we inhabit, we need the tools to craft agreements for results that will lead the way to the desired outcomes. Living in a virtual, Internet, flattened, self-managing world of free agents, with new forms of business and personal relationships, we will need new ways to express joint vision and articulate parameters and boundaries of new forms of collaboration. *In some sense the only rules of collaboration that exist are the ones you define for the particular transaction. It's* so important to have a method that will take care of collaborative transactions *because today every transaction is collaborative.*

The Book of Agreement cuts through to the core of what gets in the way of the highest levels of performance and productivity. It helps you elegantly create joint vision and quiets the internal voices of dissonance and conflict (mind chatter) that get in the way of real partnership. Max DePree (author of *Leadership Is an Art[3]* and *Leadership Jazz[4]*) was the CEO of the Herman Miller Company when it was consistently voted one of the best organizations to work for in America. He believed the success of the organization was due to *relationships based on covenant.* Agreements for results are a path to relationships based on covenant.

Summary: Formal legal agreements have their origin in the hierarchy of the feudal system. It's not surprising that power and fear are infused in the process. We're still using a way of thinking and a process derived from a historical context that is vastly different from the educated, technological world of today. The purpose of this book is to provide simple and powerful tools to arrive at *agreements for results.* You will find templates you can use as guides for crafting your own agreements. The book explores:

- The difference between *agreements for results* and *agreements for protection*
- The *ten essential elements* of agreements for results—what you need to fully discuss to create a covenant-based, heart-felt agreement
- Templates of *effective agreements* for organizational, professional, joint venture, and personal situations
- The *value of constructing agreements for results*
- The perspective of seeing the construction of agreements through authentic dialogue as *trust-generating success tools*

Understanding context is a critical part of working effectively.

Business, government, NGOs, and society in general have changed a great deal in the last fifty years. Many of the accepted norms have changed. In many places there are no norms. That's why it's critical to define norms for your unique "transaction."

Exercise: What's different about the world you live in today from the way it was ten, twenty, and thirty years ago? How are you personally impacted by the changes?

PART I

• • • • • • •

THE FOUNDATION:
LAW, PRINCIPLES, ELEMENTS, AND TEMPLATES

• • • • • • •

My personal mission is to help create cultures of agreement and resolution—places where people create *agreements for results* as part of the environment in which they live and work. A key driver for having people adopt any new set of practices is a solid foundation of principles that engage the participants and guide behavior. Chapter 1 explains and illustrates the Law of Agreement and the principles that flow from it. These are simple, undeniable truths about the way things are. Chapter 2 sets out the Ten Essential Elements that make up an effective agreement for results. Chapter 3 explains the three facets of agreement. Chapter 4 analyzes agreements for results and compares them to agreements for protection. That leads to the questions addressed in Chapter 5: What is the legal effect of agreements for results? Are they contracts? Do they work? Do they replace standard legal agreements? Chapter 6 provides an overview of the Resolutionary Model, for when the inevitable conflicts do arise.

CHAPTER 1

THE LAW OF AGREEMENT

● ● ● ● ● ● ● ●

Tis the business of little minds to shrink; but he whose heart is firm, and whose conscience approves his conduct, will pursue his principles unto death.
—Thomas Paine

Although it was almost fifteen years ago, it seems that it was yesterday when I articulated the Law and Principles of Agreement for the first time. I was so excited, you would think I had discovered a new planet or hit a lottery jackpot. I was ecstatic because I realized how fundamental agreements were to all aspects of life and how much suffering good agreements could alleviate. I also knew I would spend a good portion of the rest of my life teaching, facilitating, and writing about agreement and resolution.

I think of laws and principles as universal truths that are very difficult to refute or disprove. The *Law of Agreement* and the *Principles of Agreement* are the foundational truths on which this book is based. Like gravity, they are simple and obvious truisms that, although usually unspoken, are always present. The challenge is to stay mindful of them and to live by them. It is very important to remember that although the Law and Principles are simple to understand, they are not always easy to live by.

LAW OF AGREEMENT

• • • • •

Collaboration is established in language by making implicit (talking to yourself about what you think the agreement is) and explicit (discussing the agreement with others) agreements.

PRINCIPLES OF AGREEMENT

1. The source of productivity and fulfillment in personal and professional relationships is effective collaboration. The more seamless the collaboration, the stronger the results.

2. We work and live in a "sea" (context) of agreements.

3. We never learned the essential elements of an effective agreement.

4. Clear agreements are empowering. They express a shared vision and a road map to desired results.

5. Clear agreements improve the chances for satisfaction. They set up the conditions that produce delighted clients, customers, teammates, colleagues, vendors, and family members.

6. Practice enables you to craft masterful agreements.

7. Collaboration and agreement for results is simple, but it is not easy. It requires thoughtfulness and clear thinking on the front end, before you move into action, and a commitment to get through conflicts.

8. No matter how clear and complete the agreement, everything will not be addressed—conflicts and differences will arise that you must be prepared to resolve.

9. Breakdowns are not a cause for alarm; they are to-be-expected opportunities for creativity.

10. Resolving conflicts leads to new agreements.

Understanding the Law and Principles

THE BASIC LAW

• • • • •

Collaboration is established in language by making implicit (talking to yourself about what you think the agreement is) and explicit (discussing the agreement with others) agreements.

When we work with someone, take a job with a large organization, get married, buy someone's product, or go out for the evening with a friend, it involves coordination. Sometimes we craft long and detailed agreements with other people, such as professional sports contracts, business partnerships, or executive compensation agreements. People hire high-powered lawyers to conjure up all the things that might go wrong and all the contingencies the future might bring. They do their best to protect us from the "what ifs"—what if this goes wrong or what if that goes wrong. They try to make explicit all that they know. Unfortunately, in the name of protection, they are fostering an adversarial relationship. That is the opposite of what a new venture needs!

It takes some experience to realize that much more important than the clarity of the agreement is the quality of the relationship that develops out of reaching and working within the context of the agreement. As long as the relationship remains functional, people work things out, and the legal agreement stays in the bottom of your file drawer. The real key to the success of the collaboration is the development of relationship and trust. It's essential to make sure that everyone has the same picture, the same vision of the desired result, so that everyone is working toward making that vision the reality.

When we don't discuss the specific understanding we have with the other person or group, the agreement is *implicit.* The potential for difficulty here is that different people will have a different implicit understanding of what the agreement is. This is usually the cause of conflict.

It is an interesting phenomenon that as lawyers get older, their agreements get longer. The reason is that as lawyers becomes more experienced, the catalogue of things they have seen go wrong expands. Let's look at the principles, one by one.

*1. The source of productivity and fulfillment in
personal and professional relationships is effective
collaboration. The more seamless the collaboration,
the stronger the results.*

When you look at your life and the culture you live in, evidence abounds of this truth. You can't have an organization without the collaborative efforts of many. The arts of management and leadership are about marshaling and coordinating others' efforts. It is like conducting a great symphony. This is also true for marriages, friendships, and families. Think of the importance of effective coordination between yourself and your spouse in a highly functional marriage. Imagine that same level of collaboration in a business partnership, work team, department, or branch of an organization. When you have effective coordination, you can feel the quadratic expansion of productivity. This is called *synergy.* In any collaboration, effective end results flow from tight coordination that produces high levels of synergy. Synergy is dependent on the clarity of the shared vision and agreements we have with others.

The other critical aspect of agreements is their impact on both personal and professional relationships. Most of the satisfaction we derive in life depends on the quality of our interpersonal relationships, at home and at work. The clearer the agreement, the more satisfying the relationship. Everyone knows where they are going—no one is holding back. All of their energy is in the "game" of producing results, not fighting insignificant battles. Clearly, the opposite is also true. When the agreement is unclear, coordination is missing, productivity is greatly limited, and suffering and conflict pervade. The challenge is to be clear on the vision and desired results without needing to be specific about every facet of the project.

Aside from personal difficulties between people, much of my consulting work involves making sure everyone is operating under the same vision. Recently I helped take care of the conflict between a private agency and a department of state government. The only thing missing was a shared vision of what they were supposed to accomplish together! Conflict developed because this was not put in place at the beginning of the project. Instead, I had to do it after the fact. You can also think of an agreement as the vehicle that creates the container in which activity happens.

2. We work and live in a "sea" (context) of agreements.

You can view your life as a series of agreements. As you go through your day, try viewing your life through the "lens of agreement." From the moment you wake up to the moment you go to sleep your life is governed by the set of expectations you have as a result of the explicit and implicit agreements between you and others. You have agreements with all of the following:

- The husband or wife you share your life with
- The soldiers that protect your national borders
- The utility that supplies electricity, water, gas
- The market that sells you breakfast food

- The manufacturer of your clothing
- The municipality that provides police protection and picks up your trash
- The day care center where you leave your youngest child
- The station that services your car and sells you gasoline
- The school board that educates your children
- The company that pays your salary
- The boss you work for
- The company that services your computer
- The restaurant where you eat your lunch
- The garage where you park your car all day
- The babysitter who takes care of your kids
- The pizza shop that delivers your dinner

3. We never learned the essential elements of an effective agreement.

Although it is hard to believe, because collaboration is such a fundamental life skill, our early schooling did not include a course in effective collaboration. We never learned how to construct an effective agreement. The only way most of us get better at expressing agreements is because we suffered in the past because one of our agreements was insufficient. This makes us cautious, and sometimes mistrustful, about future collaborations, so we try to get clarity around the things that caused us trouble in the past. Unfortunately, unless we shift our way of thinking as a result of our learning or experience, we just get more paranoid and protective as time goes by.

4. Clear agreements are empowering. They express a shared vision and a road map to desired results.

When an agreement incorporates the needs, desires, and vision that each of the people involved is concerned about, you have the opportunity to express a powerful shared vision for the project. What is this collaboration about? What is the detailed picture of the result that will make everyone pleased with the outcome? It's not about you *or* me; it's about you *and* me! A clear agreement provides a road map to that vision. It details what everyone promises to do to achieve the desired result. The agreement functions to manage the project as a map that empowers and enrolls everyone in producing the joint vision. Think of the joint vision as a composite of everyone's individual vision—the vision is a "them *and* me," not a "them *or* me."

> **5. Clear agreements improve the chances for satisfaction. They set up the conditions that produce delighted clients, customers, teammates, colleagues, vendors, and family members.**

A huge amount of the suffering in this world takes place because of unclear, unarticulated, implicit agreements. In unclear situations, people don't know what to do because they don't know the results expected of them and what they can expect of others. This causes fear and anxiety. If we took the time at the beginning to express exactly where we were headed and the route of travel, everyone could rest confident, knowing the value they were expected to deliver and that the value others would deliver would take care of their needs. Everyone would know exactly what to do to fulfill their responsibilities for producing the desired end result.

Can you recall the Quaker State motor oil commercial: "You can pay me now and have your oil changed, or you can pay me much more later for costly engine repairs!" It's the same way with agreements—you can take the time at the beginning and prevent the potential of a costly hassle later on. It is that simple! Nevertheless, it is hard work to change lifelong thinking and behavioral habits.

6. Practice enables you to craft masterful agreements.

Working with any new model is challenging. Most of us want instant success. We want to take up skiing and head right for the expert slopes. We want to master that new software program quickly. We need some patience. Within a short time the agreement template becomes internalized, and you have a framework for life. After a while you will be making sure that you have effective agreements in place for all of the important aspects of your life. You will be getting good at it, and it will become easy! Be patient; allow yourself to step into "beginner's mind." Let time and experience be your teacher. You will become artful with the use of the template. Obviously, not every situation requires an explicit agreement, and not every situation requires the "religion" of a ten-element agreement. But you must start by making the basics an internalized habit.

7. Collaboration and agreement for results is simple, but it is not easy. It requires thoughtfullness and clear thinking on the front end, before you move into action, and a commitment to get through conflicts.

Periodically a state legislator will propose a law requiring more than a pulse and a blood test as requirements for a marriage license. Principle 7 makes a similar suggestion. It is a reminder that doing something effectively with another person is not easy and can become especially difficult if you don't pay attention to the details on the front end. Just as important, don't be surprised when conflicts come up that you either did not anticipate or thought were resolved.

8. No matter how clear and complete the agreement, everything will not be addressed—conflicts and differences will arise that you must be prepared to resolve.

No matter how much time you spend, no matter how perfect the attempt, you will revisit things you did not think about and circumstances you did not foresee. We can reduce conflict; we cannot eliminate it! It is important to remember that being "in the process of moving toward clear agreement" is where we spend most of our time (not at that place of perfect agreement). The goal is to normalize conflict.

The following metaphor illustrates the importance of being reconciled to the constantly evolving process of moving toward resolution and agreement. I was recently told that when you fly from New York to San Francisco, the plane is "dead on course" about 5 percent of the time. The remainder of the time, the pilot is making constant course corrections. That's the way it is. Learn to enjoy being in process. That's where we spend most of life. This is why an essential element of every agreement is a process for resolving inevitable conflicts.

The critical thing that gets you through the rough spot in any relationship is getting to the place where you have not only a meeting of the minds but also the trust that embodies a meeting of the hearts. The quality of the dialogue about the Ten Essential Elements of any agreement is designed to forge that meeting of the hearts.

9. Breakdowns are not a cause for alarm; they are to-be-expected opportunities for creativity.

Conflict and resolution are part of the same cycle. Like administrations of Republicans then Democrats, or the Dow going up then down, *breakdowns* (a stop in the action moving toward desired outcomes) are a blessing. They provide the opportunity to look at the situation with fresh eyes. From the current perspective, you have the luxury of more up-to-date information from which to act. It is critical to hold the context as one of ongoing learning as you work with an individual or a group. When things go wrong, it's not time to blame, find fault, prove yourself right, or prove them wrong. It's time to learn about what happened so you can fix the difficulty and improve the entire process for the next time you begin.

10. Resolving conflicts leads to new agreements.

Although we don't think about it from this perspective, the end result of any conflict resolution process is a new agreement determining what the relationship will be in the future. This has two important implications:

1. By taking time at the beginning of new personal and professional relationships (marriages, teams, joint ventures, employment contracts), we can prevent a great deal of suffering and conflict.

2. When conflict arises the best place to devote energy is to look to the future, and the desired results, and ask what must happen to get there. That will guide you to a new agreement. It is only useful to look at past behavior to improve the future, not to affix blame.

The goal I set for organizations with which I work is that when people get into difficulty, they can say to each other, "This is not working, is it?" They realize that the quickest way to fix the situation is to figure out what is not working about their agreement, what is incomplete about the process, or who is not doing what they are supposed to, and why? The next step is to make a new agreement and quickly let go of what was not working. The goal is to get beyond devoting any energy to drama, fault, blame or punishment. Just make a new agreement!

Summary: The basic Law of Agreement says:

Collaboration is established in language by making implicit (talking to yourself about what you think the

*agreement is) and explicit (discussing the agreement
with others) agreements.*

Understanding and embracing this fundamental truth can provide
an extremely useful perspective in our collaborations with others.

Exercise: Think about the most important working relationships
you have. Do you have a clearly articulated agreement with the
other? Do you have specifically agreed-upon outcomes and how
you will achieve them? Is your agreement written down? Have you
ever had an argument about results, method, or direction? What
was the source of the argument?

CHAPTER 2

THE TEN ESSENTIAL ELEMENTS OF EFFECTIVE AGREEMENTS

● ● ● ● ● ● ●

All you need is a plan, a road map, and the courage
to press on to your destination.
—Earl Nightingale

I hope I have convinced you of the importance and pervasiveness of agreements in your daily personal and professional life. You might be wondering how to start putting together an effective agreement. The answer is simple, but it's not easy! Simple in that all you have to do is engage in a discussion about each one of the following elements that is essential for an effective agreement. It's not easy because it means breaking lifetime habits of moving forward without putting an agreement in place. It's like shifting from

READY, **FIRE**, AIM

to

READY, **AIM**, FIRE.

A few years ago I asked a senior manager at a client company what her biggest challenge was. Without skipping a beat, she said it was getting her reports to stop and think about where they were going before they moved into action. Otherwise, they were likely to end up in places no one wanted to go.

26

Each of the following elements is an essential key for an effective agreement. Use these elements as a template for constructing agreements. It is useful to reach an understanding about each element with everyone involved. The process is very important because it is the beginning of a new working relationship. Navigating the process together is the foundation for the new relationship, which is much more important than any specific agreement. The ability to work together over time in a relationship based on covenant, no matter how difficult things are, is the context that will make the collaboration successful. One of the questions lawyers ask in determining if an agreement was legally binding is whether there was ever a meeting of the minds. I believe that to have a real agreement for results, you also need to have a meeting of the *hearts*. This is another way in which agreements for results add value.

The following words elegantly illustrate this point:

> Chaos is often the boundary of the possible, the new, and the emergent and appears to be essential to the creation of our world. Rather than trying to control and subdue chaos, we are being invited to surf the waves of change with skill and artfulness.
>
> The key to navigating the storms of turbulence cannot be found in any tool or device. The sum of our relationships will establish the overall health of our vessels and their journeys. Hence, an ethic of care and compassion for others is as fundamental as any other tool as we set out on our travels.
>
> —David La Chapelle, *Navigating the Tides of Change*

Please don't be intimidated by the template that follows. The elements become internalized quickly. Fortunately, every agreement does not require a long discussion about every element. As you use the template you will become facile with it. I encourage you to be artful, to customize it for your unique circumstances. Over the past fifteen years I have facilitated hundreds of agreements. You will be amazed at how artful you can get, both at crafting agreements and at recognizing what's missing that may lead to conflict.

The elements of an effective agreement are:

1. Intent and vision

2. Roles

3. Promises

4. Time and value

5. Measurements of satisfaction

6. Concerns, risks, and fears

7. Renegotiation/dissolution

8. Consequences

9. Conflict resolution

10. Agreement?

Here is an explanation of each element. The many examples that follow will make it clear why each element is essential.

1. *Intent and vision:* This is the big picture of what you intend to accomplish together. The first step is sharing a big picture of what you are doing together as a context for the details. The clearer and more specific the measurable detail of desired outcomes, the more likely you will attain them as visualized.

2. *Roles:* The duties, responsibilities, and commitment of everyone must be clearly defined. Everyone necessary to achieve the desired results must be part of the agreement.

3. *Promises:* The agreement contains clear promises so that everyone knows who will do what. With specific promises, you can tell if the actions will get you to the desired results and what actions are missing.

4. Time and value: All promises have deadlines for completion. These are called "by-whens"—by when will you do this and by when will you do that. The length of time the agreement will be effective is also important. Value is an understanding of who gets what for what. Is the exchange satisfactory? Is it fair? Does it provide adequate incentive? Clarity is critical because everyone must anticipate satisfaction or someone will sabotage the transaction. Remember that value has many forms, and it is essential to understand the different kinds of value people will be satisfied with.

5. Measurements of satisfaction: To prevent disagreement, the evidence that everyone has achieved his or her objectives must be clear, direct, and measurable. This element is critical because it eliminates conflict about the ultimate question—Did you accomplish what you set out to do?

6. Concerns, risks, and fears: Bringing as-yet-unspoken fears and risks to the surface provides the opportunity to anticipate and prevent some of the challenges likely to come up during the collaboration. This discussion will deepen the partnership being created, or it will let you know this is not a partnership you want. This is where you get to say what's still creating "chatter" about moving forward, and others get to respond and take care of any fear.

7. Renegotiation/dissolution: No matter how optimistic and clear you are, it will become necessary to renegotiate promises and conditions of satisfaction. Circumstances change, and it is critical to anticipate this at the beginning so the relationship can evolve and prosper. It is also crucial to provide everyone with an exit strategy that they can follow with dignity. Anyone who feels imprisoned in a transaction, partnership, or relationship cannot make his or her maximum contribution to the enterprise. It is essential to recognize that the relationship is much more important than the agreement. Things keep moving forward if the functional relationships are intact, not because of a lengthy legal contract.

8. *Consequences:* There are two kinds of consequences. Although you may not want to police the agreement, it is important to agree on consequences for anyone who breaks a promise. Equally, if not more important, it is essential to understand the consequences to everyone (including people who are not even part of the agreement) if the collaboration does not accomplish its purpose.

9. *Conflict resolution:* Conflicts and disagreements arise when people work together. If you agree to step into the attitude of resolution, and have an agreed process that leads to a new agreement, resolving conflicts will be "normalized."

10. *Agreement?* When you have dialogued about the first nine elements, it's time to ask whether you *trust* moving forward. Everyone ought to be satisfied and ready to take action. Now is the time to work on the agreement until you are satisfied that you have an agreement. If you're not clear that you do have an agreement you can trust, then you don't! Unless and until you are satisfied, do not move into action. You will not have a shared vision to work toward. Are you ready to commit to embracing the future as a new opportunity that can be enjoyed? This attitude lubricates the collaboration. Once you have agreement, someone (or everyone) must take responsibility for stewarding the project, ensuring the agreement is honored and the intended results are obtained. While this is everyone's responsibility, it is sometimes important enough to have a point person responsible for making sure the agreement is implemented. One of the questions you ask in determining if an agreement is legally binding is whether there was ever a meeting of the minds. *To have a true agreement for results, you also have to have a meeting of the hearts.*

Here's my favorite story about creating an effective agreement for results. It's my favorite because I'm very proud of the results that flowed from the agreement.

In 1999 I was called by Gail Johnson, Executive Director of

Sierra Adoption Services, a private nonprofit agency in California. A major part of the Sierra mission is working with governmental agencies by augmenting the social services they provide for children in foster care. Sierra provides extraordinary resources, beyond government capacity, so that children previously labeled "unadoptable" as a result of various disabilities can be removed from the foster care system and permanently placed in adoptive families.

Sierra was engaged in a federally funded partnership known as Capital Kids, with the appropriate social service agencies of the County of Sacramento, California. The working relationship between Sierra and Sacramento had fallen apart because of their history and because they did not have an agreement for results. The context was one of a history of conflict. Gail wanted to resolve both the long- and short-term conflict, get parties beyond their institutional mistrust, and forge an effective high-performance team. I entered a contract with the consultant engaged by the federal government to monitor the grant that was funding the Capital Kids project. Few people believed the working relationship could be salvaged.

The initial meeting included nine members from Sierra and nine from Sacramento. The first half of the day was educational. Everyone was instructed in the conversational models for collaboration and conflict resolution. After lunch I used my models to facilitate the resolution of the existing conflict. This resulted in uncovering the basis for past misunderstandings and the realization that it was possible to continue the partnership. Existing concerns were placed on the table, and a follow-up session was scheduled. At the next session, a new working agreement was structured that provided the foundation for a solid, healthy, working relationship and a new vision of partnership.

In the year following the new structure for a collaborative partnership, 109 children who had previously been considered unadoptable and destined for a life of foster care were placed in permanent adoptive homes. Here is what the Sierra Adoption

Services (SAS) agreement with Sacramento County (SC) looked like. Please take particular notice of all the operational detail. It is in the detail of behavior that "partnership" usually breaks down. That's why it's so important to take the time on the front end to pay meticulous attention to the details. The more detailed the vision, the more likely it will take place.

Capital Kids Operational Agreement

June 1999

1. *Intent and vision:* Our intention is to place as many kids as possible in permanent homes. The specific vision we have is:

- Become a model public/private partnership—a shared culture of collaboration and agreement that is seen as a role model— and teach others how we achieved it.
- Place 150 kids next year.
- SC provides 100 referrals/year to Sierra.
- Positive stories about our working relationship are generated within agencies in the adoption community.
- Sierra is accepted as a "resource" by the County.
- Sierra makes the "challenging" jobs of Suzanne and Helen do-able.
- A transfer of knowledge and resources takes place such that SC learns how to use Sierra's methods and resources.
- Funding flows easily because of the results produced.
- A high level of service is provided to clients.
- People in both agencies want to be part of the program.
- People at both agencies develop a high level of respect for each other.
- People generate a 5:1 ratio of appreciations to complaints.
- "Can't wait to go to work" attitude develops.

- A presentation about the partnership is made at NACAC.
- Partnering for performance is documented.
- High level of fun, pride, and celebration.

2. Roles: We will be partners and resources for each other. SC will look to SAS to provide resources that are beyond their capacity or ability to provide.

3. Promises:
SC will:

- Identify children to be referred for the project.
- Obtain court permission to do child-specific recruitment.
- Provide full disclosure of child's risks and needs.
- Assure County representation at referral staffing meeting, including
  — SC CapKids coordinator, long-term foster care worker and/or supervisor.
- Invite FFA worker if applicable.
- Upon request, provide waiver of confidentiality to allow SAS worker to
  — discuss child with child's therapist, FFA, Alta Regional Center, and other organizations and individuals as applicable.
  — inform current foster parent of the project.
- Facilitate SAS worker's introduction to the child and team with SAS worker as appropriate.
- Confer with SAS worker as needed re adoptive families considered for placement, including concurrence with final placement choice. Families ruled out by SAS will be reported to SC worker.
- Assure Sacramento Capital Kids liaison to attend regularly scheduled joint staff meetings to review cases, exchange feedback, remove barriers to case moving forward, review

needs and services, make new referrals, engage in dialogue necessary for project effectiveness.

- Assure that representatives will attend quarterly advisory board meetings.
- Foster Parent Adoption: (a) SAS will provide a home-study within four months. SC will provide information necessary for SAS to complete assigned foster parent home-studies. Unique situations will be processed on a case-by-case basis.
- Provide timely response to requests for documentation of placements, guardianships, and finalizations.
- Provide necessary assistance to make placement.
- Complete County requirements for adoptive placements within a reasonable time.
- Provide prompt AAP determination.
- Forward necessary documents to agency representing adopting family.
- Complete all necessary paperwork.
- Provide input for development of monthly project reports and quarterly grant progress reports.
- Participate in team-building activities and activities to identify and remove barriers.
- Participate in cross-training and joint-training activities.
- Disburse funds received from CDSS to SAS in accordance with grant budget.

SAS will:

- Provide training to SC project staff.
- Review information on children referred and accept or reject the referral within fourteen days.
- Meet with foster parents of project children to explain project and gain cooperation. If foster parent decides to adopt and SC concurs with foster parent adoption, provide home-study.

- Conduct assessment of child's adoption needs. Assessment process will consist of a minimum of:
  - Meetings with child's worker
  - Review of foster child summary, child available form, CapKids referral form, and psychological profile
  - Interviews with foster parent
  - Interviews with child
  - Interviews with other relevant individuals and organizations as applicable
- Meet with child to prepare for recruitment process.
- Facilitate photo and/or video session for the project.
- Facilitate team approach with SC worker to help child reconcile his or her past and move forward to an adoption commitment.
- Provide child-specific recruitment for each project child as necessary and as approved by juvenile court.
- Provide placement services, including:
  - Assess and report to SC all interested families.
  - Provide home-studies to appropriate families recruited to the project.
  - Solicit and review appropriate home-studies from other licensed agencies.
  - Confer with child's worker as needed re adoptive families considered for placement, including concurrence with final placement choice.
  - Interview families considered for placement.
  - Oversee preplacement visitation for children placed with SAS families.
  - Facilitate placement process for children placed with SAS families.
- In foster parent adoptions with foster families, provide a home-study within four months, and unique situations will be staffed on a case-by-case basis.

- Facilitate and attend regularly scheduled joint staff meeting with SC liaison to review cases, exchange feedback, remove barriers to case moving forward, review needs and services, make new referrals, and engage in dialogue necessary for project effectiveness.
- Attend quarterly advisory board meetings.
- Develop monthly project reports and quarterly grant progress reports with the assistance of SC liaison.
- Participate in team-building activities and activities to identify and remove barriers.
- Participate in cross-training and joint-training activities.

4. *Time and value:* We will assess our progress in six months. We agree that the effort we are devoting to this partnership is worth our time because of the potential value of finding permanent adoptive homes for the children.

5. *Measurements of satisfaction:* Placing 150 children in adoptive homes within one year.

6. *Concerns and fears:*
- We will backslide to what was unworkable.
- Each of us will be heard by the other as blaming and finding fault—in providing ongoing feedback, we either won't say the right things or we'll say the wrong things.
- People will forget forgiveness.
- We will trigger each other.
- Lack of effective feedback.
- Not enough County resources.
- Too many other demands for the project to work.
- Won't be able to place 150 kids.
- Suzanne will burn out.
- We won't be able to serve new kids.

7. Renegotiation/dissolution: We recognize that this is just the beginning of our partnership and that we will likely have to modify our practices, and this agreement, as we operate within the structure we have designed. We know that developing a working relationship on this critical mission is most important, and we agree to continue to discover the best way to do that.

8. Consequences: We understand that if we cannot work well together, many children will not be adopted into permanent families. For us, that is a huge consequence.

9. Conflict resolution: First we will talk and then we will use Stewart's seven-step Resolutionary Model. If we can't resolve things at an operational level, we will ask our senior managers to facilitate. If that does not work, we will call Stewart Levine.

10. Agreement? Yes, we are very satisfied with this new beginning.

Summary: One of the questions you ask in determining if an agreement was legally binding is whether there was ever a meeting of the minds. To have a real agreement for results, you also have to have a "meeting of the hearts."

The essential elements of an effective agreement for results are:

1. Intent and vision

2. Roles

3. Promises

4. Time and value

5. Measurements of satisfaction

6. Concerns and fears

7. Renegotiation/dissolution

   8. Consequences

   9. Conflict resolution

   10. Agreement?

Exercise: Think about one of the agreements you examined after Chapter 2. Which of the essential elements of effective agreements was not thought about or expressed? How has this missing piece affected your working relationship within the agreement you examined?

THREE FACETS OF AGREEMENT

● ● ● ● ● ● ●

When I was crossing into Gaza I was asked at the checkpoint whether
I was carrying any weapons. I replied: Oh yes, my prayer books.
—Mother Teresa

A facet is one of the many surfaces of a polished jewel that makes it shine. As you work with the elements of agreements, please remember that there are three distinct and important facets of getting to agreement. These facets are *concepts* that are as important as Mother Teresa's prayer books. Paying careful attention to the distinct importance of each facet will make your agreements shine.

1. The "Process" of Agreement

The process of agreement is the dialogue. It is the conversation in which you talk about each of the elements. The process enables you to determine if shared vision and trust are present. If you find that a shared vision and a sense of trust are present, you feel comfortable declaring that you have an agreement. If trust or shared vision is absent, it's wise to avoid the mistake of moving the project forward, and much better to do something else! During the process, the dialogue surfaces all the details of the project, the trust level you have with others, the real value of the transaction to you, and whether you believe moving forward is worth it. As a result of this collaborative dialogue, a relationship and a joint vision for the future are designed, or not! This is where the covenant is created and a meeting of the hearts is established.

2. The "Phenomenon" of Agreement

When you complete the agreement process, you have a shared vision for the future. If you are honest and open, and you do a good job of communicating, hearts and minds are joined together in a covenental relationship focused on producing a certain result. The barometer for this is your feeling about whether you believe you have an agreement that you trust. If you do not trust that this phenomenon is present, you are not ready to move the relationship forward. Agreements for results are a path to relationships based on covenant.

These heartfelt connections, whether the context is business or personal, reflect the essence of our humanity and what we are all hungry for, although we have been conditioned otherwise. Remember that the tenth essential element of an agreement for results is "Agreement?" You must ask yourself after the dialogue process if you are comfortable moving forward. If yes, you have an agreement; if not, you don't. The greatest trouble can be caused when you move forward when there is doubt. *Please don't do it!*

3. The "Artifact" of Agreement

When the phenomenon of agreement is present, it is smart to put the essence of the covenants in writing. This will act as a guide as you move forward with the relationship. Remember that if the relationship remains intact, whatever artifact you put together will remain on the shelf, in the drawer, or in cyberspace! As long as a solid relationship has been created, you will be able to work through the difficult spots without pulling out the artifact.

When things get stuck, you'll need the seven-step process of the Resolutionary Model as presented in Chapter 6. This will get you through any breakdowns that may impede your reaching the joint vision of results expressed in your agreement.

An Agreement for Results

After fifteen years of running his own consulting and training business, John decided to take a position as the executive director of a regional learning center to be called Learning, Inc. (LI). LI will be an NGO whose board is made up of members of for-profit organizations, school boards, universities, and government and community representatives. John wanted a clear vision of where they were headed. He wanted to know where he was headed, how he would get there, and the metrics by which his success or failure would be evaluated. John engaged in a dialogue with the board. The following agreement is the framework for John's employment. Notice the detail of the vision.

1. Intent and vision: To build a leading-edge, state-of-the-art conference and learning center. The facility will be booked one year in advance; it will be featured in three national training magazines; requests will be received from large corporate universities to use the design as a model; the physical design will win awards; technology and distance learning will be state-of-the-art; the operation will be financially self-sustaining; working on the project will be inspiring; the metrics used to measure learning will reveal that the physical facility greatly enhanced the level of learning; the facility is used by the local community, including the local government and the local corporate community; the facility is always a work in progress; relationships are collegial; part of the operation is funded by government and foundation grants, part by corporate entities, and part by local government.

2. Roles: John is the executive director who will function as a conductor; the board representing stakeholder groups will be advisors. Also needed will be fundraisers, design professionals, corporate sponsors, government sponsors, students, educators, contractors, politicians, the media, responsive and engaged community members, and volunteers.

3. Promises: John promises to listen to the vision of the advisory council and bring it into being, to devote full time to the venture, to do whatever it will take to make the vision a reality by engaging the professionals and community in a building and fundraising process, and to see the project as a learning exercise. The board promises to pay John's salary, support his efforts, provide the input he needs, be available to listen, and be receptive to new ideas.

4. Time and value: The project will be built within six years and John agrees to stay engaged until it is up and running and for at least three years after that. John will be satisfied with $75,000 per year for two years and a raise of $10,000 per year after that. John acknowledges that a high level of satisfaction will come from getting the project launched.

5. Measurements of satisfaction: Critical benchmarks will be the ability to accommodate 2,000 students, operating surplus of $300,000 per year, endowment of $100 million, visitors from foreign countries, volunteers, and realizing the specific vision.

6. Concerns and fears: Conflict between advisory committee members, conflict between advisory committee members and John, lack of funds, and loss of commitment.

7. Renegotiation: Anything is open to renegotiations at any time. John can leave at his sole discretion after three years.

8. Consequences: If John leaves before three years, he loses three months' compensation. If the project does not get built, the community loses a great potential hub.

9. Conflict resolution: We agree to use the models and principles found in Getting to Resolution.

10. Agreement? Yes, we have an agreement. John is responsible for moving the project forward.

This was the first time John participated in the process of creating an agreement for results. Because the experience proved so valuable for John, he has facilitated agreements with each of his department heads, and they in turn have done so for each of their directors.

Summary: There are three important aspects of agreements to keep in mind: (1) the "process" of agreement is the negotiation and exchange of information; (2) the "phenomenon" of agreement is a meeting of the minds by which you can comfortably say "yes, I trust we have an agreement"; and (3) the "artifact" of agreement is the writing that expresses what has been agreed to. To have an effective agreement you can implement and use as a structure to frame collaborative activity, all three are necessary.

Exercise: Please recall a collaboration that was not effective. Which one of the three critical aspects of agreement were missing? How might the presence of that aspect of agreement have impacted the collaboration?

CHAPTER 4

THE NEW MINDSET:
AGREEMENTS FOR RESULTS

● ● ● ● ● ● ●

We shall turn from the soft voices in which a civilization decays.
We shall return to the stern virtues by which a civilization is made.
We shall do this because, at long last, we know that we must,
because finally we begin to see that the hard way is the only enduring way.
—Walter Lippmann

It is much easier not to exercise or brush your teeth in the morning; it is much simpler just to get on with your day. I quote Walter Lippmann as a reminder that although stopping to form an agreement before moving forward is more tedious than moving into action immediately, it will likely produce enduring results.

When introducing the concept of *agreements for results* to an audience, I always talk about the tag line from the Quaker State motor oil commercial: *You can pay me now, or you can pay me later.* That line holds true when thinking about agreements. Most people never think about investing the time to make explicit the implicit agreement they believe they have at the beginning of a new personal or professional relationship, team, or project. They're off and running, everyone with their own vision of the destination and how to get there, without the clarity necessary to minimize the potential for conflict. Like the Quaker State warning of engine damage, if you don't do the preventive maintenance of changing your oil, you will incur the cost of inevitable conflict, a cost that will be much greater and that likely could have been prevented.

When we think about the idea of having an *agreement,* we usually think about long legal documents, extensive adversarial negations, lots of "what ifs," and how we can protect ourselves from something we do not want to happen. I was brainwashed as a young lawyer. I was taught that a good lawyer is paid to become paranoid and worry about all the things that might go wrong. That was the mindset I was taught to step into when "protecting" clients. At some point I realized that it was just as important to focus on helping clients achieve results, and that if I was an overzealous protector, I was not serving my client.

This book suggests a paradigm that shifts the focus to a vision of results people want to produce, not the calamities they want to avoid. This chapter explains the differences between the old and new perspective.

Comparison: Agreements for Results and Agreements for Protection

	Results Focus	*Protection Focus*
Intent and vision	Desired outcome	What ifs
Roles	Take responsibility	Limit accountability
Promises	Commitment	Qualifiers and conditioners
Time and value	By whens/fair return	Most for least
Measurements of satisfaction	Inspiring goals	Excuses and escapes
Concerns and fears	Compassion/ understanding	Edge for strategic advantage
Renegotiation	Deal with unknowns/changes	Strike hard bargain
Consequences	Reminder of promises	Punishment
Conflict resolution	Get back on track	Exact some premium
Agreement ?	Trust enough	Escape possible?

Agreements for Results and
Agreements for Protection Explained

1. *Intent and vision*

> **Results:** Focusing on what you want to happen
>
> **Protection:** Focusing on all the "what-ifs" that could go wrong

You can tell what will happen in your life by paying attention to your dominant thoughts. Given that, if we focus on the calamities, we increase the chances they will happen. What we really want in any collaborative context is everyone focusing on desired results—the best possible vision of future results. That will greatly improve the chances that what we want to materialize will happen. It's obvious that when you bring on a new hire, it's more useful to see them leaping tall buildings than worrying and focusing on the mistakes they might make. Empowering outcomes is the purpose of agreements for results.

2. *Role*

> **Results:** Making sure someone has responsibility for all critical tasks
>
> **Protection:** Narrowly defining responsibility to limit accountability and liability

We want to make sure we have what we need to get the job done without anything slipping through the cracks. We want clarity about who can be counted on for what so we don't have someone saying, "That's not my job!" In the old context, people liked to hide. They did not like to take responsibility for making something happen because if something went wrong, they were responsible. We hope that the fear of making mistakes is no longer as powerful a driver as it once was. We have all learned that the need for innovation requires experimentation. We know that mistakes cannot be "punished" if you expect continued risking, which is the heart of entrepreneurship.

3. Promises

> ***Results:*** Contribution; committing wholeheartedly to do your part required for success, not out of coercion but from belief in the project's mission

> ***Protection:*** Doing the least; hiding behind qualifying words that cloud and condition what you are promising

Who, specifically, will be doing what? Consider this a project management plan. This is also a checkpoint: If everyone delivers what he or she promises, will you produce the desired results? Each promise must have the discipline of a "by when," because without a date, commitment is illusory.

4. Time and value

> ***Results:*** Clear time commitments and satisfaction with the value given and received

> ***Protection:*** The most for the least

Clearly state "by whens" and for how long the promises will be kept. Everyone must be satisfied that what they will get from the project is worth what they are putting in. If someone is undercompensated, they will be resentful. Resentful participants do not produce results that are beyond expectation, but people committed to a vision do.

5. Measurements of satisfaction

> ***Results:*** Goals that inspire and state clearly and measurably what is expected

> ***Protection:*** Qualifiers to argue from and use as excuses

What are the objective measures that will tell you if you accomplished what you set out to do in a way that there are no arguments about it? For some people it is frightening to make a commitment that will hold them accountable to a promise they made, so they will look for an edge.

6. Concerns and fears

> **Results:** Compassion for any anxiety-producing concerns and risks that a partner sees and feels

> **Protection:** An edge to take strategic advantage of when you are inside their head, in a position to play "games"

You address concerns and fears to make everyone as comfortable as possible about moving forward. Doing this is a way of responding to internal chatter that might inhibit full participation. It solidifies partnership by addressing what is lingering in people's minds. It enables people to identify risks clearly and to choose to move forward anyway. Each person should be willing to take the other's deal.

7. Renegotiation

> **Results:** How can we make this work as unanticipated changes take place?

> **Protection:** How can changes be used for advantage?

A commitment to renegotiation requires ongoing learning and staying in the mindset of solving a mutual problem to get desired results even though things happened that no one anticipated (one thing you can be sure of!). This is the key principal that drives every learning organization. When you are in a protection mindset, the analysis is about who gains the advantage in the changed circumstances; it becomes more about winning than having the project achieve desired results.

8. Consequences

> *Results:* What reminds everyone of the significance of promises and failure?

> *Protection:* What would be a good punishment?

It is important to keep people mindful of promises they made and focused on delivering what they promised. It is just as important to have people realize the connection between their expectations and their failure to perform. Becoming conscious of that gap serves as a motivator. Consequences are put in place not as punishment but to remind us of the loss of an unrealized vision and the sanctity of our promises.

9. Conflict resolution

> *Results:* What will get us back on track quickly?

> *Protection:* How can the resolution process be used for leverage or advantage?

It is important to embrace conflict as to be expected and to hold it as an opportunity for creativity in the way we deal with specifics we did not anticipate. It is very important to understand the magnitude of the transaction cost of remaining in conflict. It is important to realize that in many situations, fomenting conflict and prolonging it are part of a chosen business strategy. It is critical to understand this early on so you don't waste your energy.

10. Agreement?

> *Results:* Do I *trust* enough to be in an open, ongoing collaboration?

> *Protection:* Can I get out without getting hurt? Is there an opportunity for a windfall?

Has the process produced enough *trust* so you can say, "Let's do it, I'm comfortable moving forward with you, and I sense we'll be able to work things out as we go forward"? Has the deep dialogue we have exchanged produced what Max DePree calls a relationship based on covenant—a heartfelt connection and commitment to people and results?

An Agreement for Results

I recently facilitated a new business partnership agreement among three women who had an extraordinary idea. Because of their unique individual circumstances, the situation held great potential for the three women to step into a desire for protection that would foster competition. The scenario involved an untested idea whose viability was difficult to assess, great disparity in present financial needs, and different track records. They were progressive in their thinking and approached me after hearing me speak.

They were a joy to work with—openly appreciative of a positive approach, committed, enthusiastic, and focused on the vision of what they wanted to produce. Usually I'm the one who keeps reminding others of their vision, but in this situation vision was pulling them forward like a magnet. I will use their experience to illustrate the new paradigm of partnership based on an *agreement for results* model.

The women approached me because they believed I could help get them through the major differences that concerned them while honoring the value of and preserving their important personal relationships. Because they had limited resources, I let them do a lot of the work and functioned as a coach. I explained the model and sent them away to work through it and present me with a first try at their agreement. I am very pleased to report that with a moderate amount of guidance, they did a good job at structuring a way for them to move forward. They were quickly able to put in place an agreement for results that they never would have arrived at with a traditional lawyer (more likely three lawyers, as each of them would need representation because of technical conflict-of-interest concerns). If you want to compare this with an agreement for protection, look at the standard clauses in the automobile sales agreement in Chapter 10. Here's the agreement they drafted.

Agreement

1. Intent and vision: Joan, Alicia, and Patricia, close personal friends, each currently running our own businesses, want to form a venture that will be a model for women in business together. We want this venture to be highly profitable while at the same time being a new model of personal business relationship. Our intention is to design, manufacture, and sell a line of woman's leisure clothing that will be unlike anything on the market.

2. Roles: We will be collaborators who work in business and at the same time preserve our very important personal relationships. Joan will be in charge of finance and raising capital. Alicia will be the master of design and creativity. Patricia will be responsible for sales and marketing, finding outlets for the clothing. We will continue to be close personal friends as we explore the boundaries of combined business and personal relationships.

3. Promises: We each promise to devote approximately one-third of our time to this joint venture. We promise to be concerned and responsive to the nonbusiness needs and concerns of each other. Within three months, Joan promises to secure $1 million in financing and Alicia promises to design a full line of playclothes, twenty-four separate designs suitable for presentation to investors. Patricia promises to secure $300,000 worth of orders within three months from the date designs are presented. We promise to collaborate with each other about all business decisions worth more than $1,000. We promise to listen, learn, and take care of each other's emotional needs during the ordinary course of business. We promise to rent modest (less than $1,000/month) office space within the month, each one of us supplying what we can by way of furniture. Of critical importance: *We promise to laugh, a lot!*

4. *Time and value:* We have no doubt our business will be highly profitable. We each agree to make an initial capital contribution of $10,000, which will be returned once financing is secured. We will devote full time to the business for the next month. We have no question that this venture will make a significant financial return. We will review the status of the business in six-month intervals.

5. *Measurements of satisfaction:* We will be satisfied if each of us can take $1,000 per week from the business after the first year. We would like to retire our debt within five years. Because of the personal contact in the business, we will each be very happy to be working with each other. We agree that if that is not so, we will end the business.

6. *Concerns and fears:* We fear that the business will fail and that in the process our personal relationships will be destroyed. We are all concerned that any one of us may take advantage of our friendship and not put in the required effort.

7. *Renegotiation:* We understand that relationship is about constant renegotiation. That is the part we want to learn how to do well. Seamless, daily interaction and renegotiation with each other, without anger or resentment, is part of the learning and value we are striving for.

8. *Consequences:* Because we have been talking about our venture in our community, we see a great risk of loss of reputation, face, and friendship. If any of us breaks a promise to the other, we will donate $10 to the UNICEF Children's Relief Fund.

9. Conflict resolution: We will talk and talk and talk. If we can't facilitate for each other, we will get another person to help. We will call Stewart if we get stuck.

10. Agreement? Yes, we are excited about moving forward together.

In the new partnership, one woman was the creative driver, one was the marketing person, and the third was responsible for finance and operations. Promises were made about creative design deadlines, securing investors, sales strategy, and sales goals. Because of different needs, an agreement was reached about different levels of initial compensation for each partner. It was also agreed that after six months the three would evaluate how things were going. For the three women, satisfaction had three components: product in the world, income, and the continuing viability of their personal relationships.

One lingering concern had to be addressed. It involved a concern about an earlier personal behavior that could destroy the partnership. Because it surfaced, it was responded to. That cleared the air and allayed the fear of moving forward. It was agreed that ongoing dialogue was essential for viability. I was consulted to help with difficult concerns that were not predicted. We used contributions to charity for broken promises. A triage was put in place for resolving conflict: talk, talk to a mutual friend, and talk to Stewart. And, ultimately, it was agreed that the process had built a joint vision, a relationship, and a partnership based on covenant.

Summary: There is an important difference between agreements for results and agreements for protection. Protective agreements, the current standard paradigm, focus on the "what ifs" and how to protect against them. The primary inquiry is about what will take place if this or that disaster occurs. In the new paradigm, agreements for results focus on the vision that brought people or organizations together. What is the desired result, and what do we have to do to make it happen?

Exercise: Find a written agreement that you have with someone. This could be for the purchase of a home or automobile, or the agreement you have with a credit card or mortgage company. As you look through the agreement, notice whether each provision seeks to protect or articulate where you are headed and how you will get there. If you have other agreements handy, examine them too.

CHAPTER 5

ARE THEY LEGALLY BINDING CONTRACTS?

• • • • • • •

The practice of law consists of whatever a lawyer does.
—Carl Llewellen, *The Bramble Bush*

The most frequently asked questions I get are: (1) whether agreements for results are legally binding contracts; (2) whether legalese is a required part of a contract; (3) what to do if I need protection, especially in a commercial situation; and (4) whether my lawyer can learn to do this. Answers: yes, no, maybe, and maybe.

Agreements for Results Are Legally Binding Contracts

"My name is Stewart and I am a lawyer!" (Even after twenty years in "recovery.") The following opinion is proof that I'm a lawyer because this is what lawyers do—they render opinions, and here I am opining. So even after twenty years in recovery, I am still, and will always be, a lawyer. When I first started drafting agreements for results, I was afraid I was going to be disbarred, arrested, or accused of treason. The idea of making up something on your own, without precedent or following a form book, is so foreign to the legal context! But that's why most lawyers have difficulty being creative—they look to the past to decide what is appropriate for the future. That is the antithesis of Albert Einstein's warning that we would not be able to solve current problems with current levels of thinking. After a while, given the Resolutionary I am, I transcended the fear, especially when people started reporting their results.

Although someone might argue otherwise, it is safe to say that for our purposes the terms *agreements* and *contracts* have the same meaning. The essential requirement for an agreement to be legal is that it be legally enforceable. That means you can go to court and have the court order someone to keep their promise or pay you compensation for their failure. (I note how quickly I can feel myself slipping into the language of lawyers even after twenty years of recovery!)

That means that if John promises to build a barn for Mary, Mary promises to pay John $2,000 upon completion, and John builds the barn, then he can sue Mary to collect regardless of whether the price was fair. Although courts are concerned with the existence of consideration (you must give something to get something), they are not concerned with the adequacy of consideration, whether it was a fair deal.

If an agreement for results contains a promise by one person to do something by a certain date, for a certain amount, and the promised performance can be measured, then it is a legally enforceable agreement. From a legal perspective, all of the other language in an agreement for results was nice to have, but it's not legally essential to enforceability. A court interpreting an agreement for results would think of that language as precatory—nice wishes, but not legally enforceable.

Legalese Is Not Required

Legalese is definitely not required to make something "legal" or official. Historically, legal doctrine did require certain specific words in legal documents like deeds, contracts, and court pleadings. Those days have long passed, and most legalese is left over from the past and of no significance, although it can still be found on some legal forms. In some ways, legalese demonstrates laziness about cleaning up old language. Some states have actually passed "plain language" legislation requiring documents to be in plain English.

Protection Permissible

Agreements for results can be filled with protection. When people have concerns or fears, you can provide protection. Consequences for failure to do something are certainly a form of protection. Protection against a real fear is not a bad thing. What gets in the way of moving forward with a degree of good faith is primarily approaching the situation from a perspective of trying to "win" by being completely protected and safe. That will never create the kind of covenantal working partnership that can produce great results. Another significant point to remember is that the existing bodies of both statutory and case law become an implied part of your agreement. This supplies all kinds of legalese you are not even aware of, but it is there to protect you

It's interesting that people ask these questions and that the answers are clear. In fact, once people begin working inside of the context of agreements for results, questions about legality and enforceability don't come up, and I'm not surprised. As I've said, the real value in having the agreement is not its legal effect; the value is in developing the relationship through dialogue. Participating authentically in the dialogue process results in the legality of the agreement taking on secondary, or no, importance. People are thinking much more about responsibilities, results, value, service, and participation than about rights. The relationship endures and prospers while the written agreement collects dust. Why do you think the contracts of great sports figures are routinely revised after stellar performances. The relationship is much more important—validating, honoring, continuing, and preserving it.

Training Your Lawyer

I'm often asked if people can train their lawyer to prepare agreements for results. The answer is maybe. The answer is informed by my own paranoia that I was doing something terribly wrong when I first invented the idea and started doing something different. Your lawyer will have to overcome the following obstacles to become masterful at agreements for results:

- The mind set of looking to precedent for permission and authority. Lawyers are trained to look to the past for validation of a proposed action. That's why I was "seasick" when I first started using them.

- It's not in the legal form book and I can't make it up myself; let's rely on the legal publishers. Yes, that would be a lawyerly response. It reflects the fear of independent thinking that would allow you to apply principles you know to give yourself permission.

- *Right/wrong, win/lose, fault/blame* are essential parts of the legal mindset.

- Lawyers are not supposed to get involved with the business deal. They just legalize a done deal presented to them.

- Ethics require zealous representation; therefore, I might be committing malpractice. This is a lawyer's major concern. It reflects a protection mentality.

- These results-based agreements come out of values other than protecting property.

Most resistance comes from the mindset developed by current professional training. *Good luck!*

Having said that, I can also report a great deal of progressive thinking within the legal community. Movements like restorative justice, lawyers as problem solvers, renaissance lawyers, holistic lawyers, and contemplative law retreats are happening.

In part, these movements are springing up because most lawyers are unhappy with their practice—because of who it requires them to be and what it requires them to do.

Recently I presented the Resolutionary Model and agreements for results to a group of senior defense attorneys, usually thought of as conservative and resistant to new thinking. The gentleman who invited me said that I had won the minds and hearts of the audience. So there is hope!

Summary: Agreements for results are legally binding contracts as long as they contain an identifiable promise to perform some service or deliver merchandise of some kind and a promise of some form of consideration in return. Legalese is not required. Agreements for results can and do include elements of protection.

Exercise: Think about a current situation that is causing you stress, the sign that you have a conflict that needs attention. Prepare two agreements that address the situation, an agreement for results and an agreement for protection. Which one would you rather be part of? Meet with the other people and see which one they are more eager to participate in.

CHAPTER 6

WHEN CONFLICT SURFACES:
THE RESOLUTIONARY MODEL

● ● ● ● ● ● ●

The essence of resolving conflict can be boiled down to two words—listening
and forgiveness. If you do these two things well, the rest is easy.
—The Resolutionary

Let's take another look at Principle 8:

8. No matter how clear and complete the agreement,
everything will not be addressed—conflicts and
differences will arise that you must be prepared to
resolve.

No matter how much time you spend, no matter how close to perfect the attempt, you will have to revisit aspects of the agreement
that you did not think about, or changed circumstances you did
not contemplate. Although you can reduce conflict, you cannot
eliminate it! Getting emotional about conflict will not help resolve
it. Just as with a template for reaching agreement, you will find the
Resolutionary Model for conflict resolution very helpful. This
chapter provides a good overview of that model. Although both
The Book of Agreement and *Getting to Resolution* can stand alone,
they are intimately entwined. They express different points on the
same Cycle of Resolution.

Cycle of Resolution

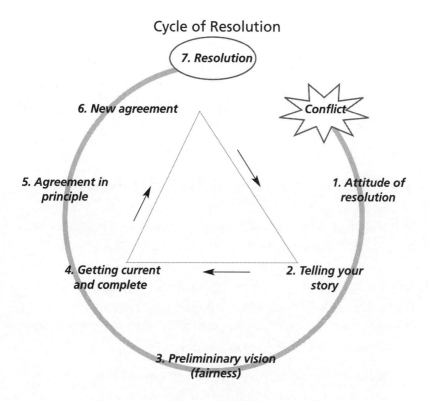

7. Resolution

6. New agreement

Conflict

5. Agreement in
principle

1. Attitude of
resolution

4. Getting current
and complete

2. Telling your
story

3. Prelimininary vision
(fairness)

Resolution is essential, not only after you begin the collaboration but also for conflict that comes up in the process of forming the initial collaborative agreement. The Seven Resolutionary Steps will surface what's behind a position so agreement can be reached. The steps of the Resolutionary Model are:

Step 1. Developing the attitude of resolution

Step 2. Telling your story

Step 3. Listening for a preliminary vision of resolution

Step 4. Getting current and complete

Step 5. Seeing a vision for the future: agreement in principle

Step 6. Crafting the new agreement: making the vision into reality

Step 7. Resolution: when your agreement becomes reality

Although I have referred to these as seven distinct steps, they are not linear. Some reflect a mental set, whereas others involve doing. But thinking—particularly what and how we think—is an activity; it is something we can choose to do a certain way. Steps 1, 3, 5, and 7 are more about a mental model. Steps 2, 4, and 6 require action. Here are the seven steps.

Step 1. Developing the Attitude of Resolution

The ten principles that make up the Attitude of Resolution hold the values of a new way to think about conflict. This attitude is the place of beginning, a critical first step of getting to resolution. This will not happen at once. It will take time to change the way you think. This is a foundational step. The goal is to internalize the principles, and that will happen over time. Here are the principles that make up the Attitude of Resolution:

Believing in abundance—there is enough for everyone

Efficiency—being mindful of the costs of continued conflict

Creativity—focusing on solutions

Fostering resolution—will the process get you there?

Openness—telling your truth

Long-term perspective—thinking about tomorrow and future impact on relationships

Honoring feelings—knowing it's about more than logic

Disclosure of information—keeping no secrets

Learning—listening, being educated by the process, and being willing to shift positions

Responsibility—taking personal responsibility for the resolution

Step 2. Telling Your Story

The second step is telling your story and listening to all the stories, including yours. It is about understanding and being understood. If you learn to listen with a careful ear and honor everyone's story about a situation, you take a big step toward getting to resolution.

Step 3. Listening for a Preliminary Vision of Resolution

The third step is to start thinking about a resolution that honors all concerns in the situation. It is about shifting from the desire to win (get your own way) to a vision that everyone can buy into. It comes from a sense of fairness. This initial vision may change as you gather more information and learn more.

Step 4. Getting Current and Complete

The fourth step demands saying difficult, sometimes gut-wrenching things. It is about articulating what usually goes unexpressed and escaping from the emotional and intellectual prisons that keep us locked in the past. It is a way to face the good and bad in any situation and to experience and grieve for the disappointment of unrealized expectations. It is a way to put all of the detail out on the table—and choose those remnants that can be used to weave a new tapestry of resolution.

Step 5. Seeing a Vision for the Future: Agreement in Principle

Now that you have a preliminary vision, along with the information and emotional freedom provided by the completion process, you are ready for the fifth step—reaching an agreement in princi-ple. Having looked at what other people need and noticing the cracks in your righteous position, you are ready to reach a general understanding of the resolution. This is the foundation of a new agreement. You let go of the desire for what you know will not work, and you focus on what will. This is the first part of building a new future.

Step 6. Crafting the New Agreement: Making the Vision into Reality

In the sixth step you put specifics onto the agreement in principle. You design and construct a detailed vision of the future. You have a map, a formula for the dialogue, that will maximize the potential for everyone to obtain their desired results. The more time you spend in detailing the desired results, the greater the chance to realize them.

Step 7. Resolution: When Your Agreement Becomes Reality

The seventh and final step is moving back into action. With a new agreement and a quiet, clear mind about the past, you can freely move forward, devoting your energy and intention to currently desired outcomes. You will have a new and profound sense of free-dom because you have spoken all the unspeakables. You have completed the past and constructed a clear picture of the future and of the path that will get you there. You will be empowered by the process. You are resolved. It's important to make note of the *quality* of the resolution. The resolution you have come to is not a compromise or settlement in which everyone gives in. The resolu-tion is an agreement for results that was forged from the opportu-nity that conflict always presents. It is the opposite of what I heard at the courthouse as a young lawyer: that you know you have a good settlement when everyone is unhappy!

The seven steps provide a context for the model to be integrated into the realities of a larger whole, that can be used when breakdowns become problematic, either in forming the initial agreement or once the collaboration begins. The critical thing to remember is that when a breakdown occurs, the resolution is a new agreement. The key is always to focus on the desired outcome, the vision for the future, not the "problem" of the conflict. If you want a fuller explanation of the Resolutionary process, you can find it in *Getting to Resolution.*

Summary: Principle 8 says

> *8. No matter how clear and complete the agreement, everything will not be addressed—conflicts and differences will arise that you must be prepared to resolve.*

Though you can reduce conflict, you cannot eliminate it! Getting emotional about conflict will not help resolve it. Just as with a template for reaching agreement, you will find the Seven-Step Resolutionary Model for conflict resolution very helpful, either after the collaboration begins or in getting to agreement. The goal is to normalize the conflict that does arise.

The steps of the model are:

Step 1. Developing the attitude of resolution

Step 2. Telling your story

Step 3. Listening for a preliminary vision of resolution

Step 4. Getting current and complete

Step 5. Seeing a vision for the future: agreement in principle

Step 6. Crafting the new agreement: making the vision into
   reality

Step 7. Resolution: when your agreement becomes reality

Exercise: Think about a breakdown in a current working relation-ship that you have not been able to resolve on your own. Try the Seven-Step Resolutionary Model. First use the model yourself and allow it to surface the parts of the situation that are yours. Then bring in the others who are involved.

PART II

• • • • • • •

ORGANIZATIONAL APPLICATIONS

• • • • • • •

The larger organizations are, the greater the need for coordination and collaboration. As organizations flatten, management hierarchies disappear, dotted-line reporting relationships proliferate, cross-functional teams emerge, virtual organizations and contract employees become the norm, and having a structure to define relationships becomes increasingly important. Part II provides a broad spectrum of agreements that will help individuals design effective collaborations inside and between organizations. Most of the agreements are practical (for example, employment and sales agreements). Some are aspirational, like agreements between corporations and the communities they inhabit. I hope you will find them useful.

CHAPTER 7

EMPLOYMENT RELATIONSHIPS

● ● ● ● ● ● ●

Anything on earth you want to do is play.
Anything on earth you have to do is work.
Play will never kill you, work will.
I never worked a day in my life.
—Leila Denmark, on her 102nd birthday

A few years ago, in the height of the high-tech boom, I was working with an organization whose newly minted managers were not performing up to par. I suspected that the phenomenon was widespread, given how hot the segment of the economy was and the lack of time for training new managers. An official from the Bureau of Labor Statistics told me that in the previous six months, 250,000 new managers had lost their jobs within six months of being promoted. She told me that the bureau became concerned, so they polled the terminated employees. They found that most employees were terminated for poor performance. When the interviewers probed more deeply, they found that performance was poor because *employees did not know what their job was and what was expected of them.*

In the flattening world of knowledge workers, projects are much more collegial than hieratical. That said, there is still usually someone identified as the boss. When I teach management seminars, one of my favorite and most revealing exercises involves asking participants to reflect on two questions:

69

1. What does your supervisor expect of you?

2. What do you expect of your supervisor?

My message to students is: If you don't have a solid sense of the answer to these questions, the first thing you should do tomorrow is to have dialogues with your supervisor and with all of your direct reports. I suggest following the agreement template to structure your employment relationship. In some instances this involves stating the obvious, while in others it reveals critical information.

The Ten Element template for agreements that I introduced in Chapter 3 is easy to follow. It's not necessary to have a facilitator. It's a matter of getting clear about expectations. Here is an agreement between the executive director of an adoption agency and one of her department heads. I suggest that all managers who have others reporting to them keep blank templates around because situations where agreements are valuable come up all the time. As you look at this agreement, and the ones that follow, notice that the amount of detail will vary with the circumstance.

Employment Agreement

1. Intent and vision: Our intention is to have a collaborative employment relationship that is focused on the mission of our organization—moving kids out of foster care and finding permanent homes for them. John's vision is that he will run his department on his own without daily input and micromanaging from Rita, that Rita will provide mentoring and consultation when needed, that Rita will groom John for her job, and that Rita will provide ongoing feedback. Rita's vision is that John will run his department independently with no need for daily contact or supervision, that John reach his annual placement goals and quarterly benchmarks, that John manage the fifteen people reporting to him without the need for her intervention, and that John and his department will contribute to the agency's culture of collaboration.

2. *Roles:* Rita is a resource, mentor, coach, and teacher. John is responsible for his department. John and Rita agree that for their operation to be successful they will need the support of other departments, a supply of kids and adoptive parents, and the cooperation of legal authorities and the media.

3. *Promises:*

John promises: To stay focused on the goal of the agency; to keep his emotions in check; to seek guidance before situations become problems; to advise Rita of situations that may become problems; to keep his spending within budget; not to be overzealous in advocating for a particular child; to prepare agreements for each person in his department; to be enrolled continually in some form of education or self-improvement.

Rita promises: To let John run his department; to always be available as a resource; to provide the funds needed for John's department and to keep the organization running; to resolve any conflicts between John's department and other operating units; to be honest in her conversations with John; to meet with John monthly and provide detailed feedback.

4. *Time and value:* John and Rita agree that they will honor this agreement for one year, at which time they will review their working relationship. They agree that they will keep renewing it for one-year periods after their annual review and modification. John is satisfied with the value he receives, which includes his salary and perks, and the satisfaction of placing children. John would like annual increases of between 5 and 10 percent of his current earnings. If John keeps his promises, Rita will be satisfied with the value she receives for what she must give. This is true for her personally and for the organization in her capacity as ED.

5. *Measurements of satisfaction:* The measure of satisfaction will be (1) the placement of 120 children for the year and the benchmarks leading up to that; and (2) a positive rating of 80 percent of organizational employees in the annual employee satisfaction survey.

6. *Concerns and fears:* Rita is concerned that John will not be able to control his temper. John is concerned about Rita providing enough funding.

7. *Renegotiation:* John and Rita agree to be open to modifying this agreement at any time. They understand that their ongoing relationship, and their ability to work together, is more important than the details of this agreement. They agree that if either one of them is not happy with their working relationship, they will negotiate a change before engaging in destructive behavior.

8. *Consequences:* John and Rita understand that if their relationship does not work effectively, kids deserving of families will remain in foster care. If John or Rita breaks a promise, they agree to make a $10 donation to their favorite charity. The determination of broken promises will be made by Anthony, a member of their board.

9. *Conflict resolution:* John and Rita agree to the following triage in resolving any conflict between them: (1) they will talk with each other; they will not focus on the problem, but on the vision they have for effective collaboration; (2) they will ask Anthony for help; (3) they will engage a managerial mediator; (4) they will engage an arbitrator to decide.

10. *Agreement?* John and Rita have reached a place of trust and say they have an agreement they can live with and flourish within—not so much the written words, but the relationship created by the dialogue that led to this agreement. They will both manage this agreement to achieve the results it envisions.

There is no "right" way to do this. The critical action is to do it. Having the dialogue is a fundamental step in creating a sustainable relationship even when circumstances are difficult. The dialogue is the context for creating a meeting of the minds and hearts. It is much more important than any writing. Clients report that using this practice in their organization generates productivity gains because people are more secure in their relationship with their supervisor.

Summary: Often employees have trouble with their job because they do not know what their job is and what is expected of them. Two questions every employee and every supervisor must ask themselves are:

1. What does your supervisor expect of you?

2. What do you expect of your supervisor?

If you don't have a solid sense of the answer to both questions, it is critical to engage in the "process" of establishing an agreement with your supervisor.

Exercise: Establish an "employment agreement for results" with your manager, the person responsible for your coaching and development, and with all of your direct reports if you have management responsibility.

CHAPTER 8

SENIOR EXECUTIVE TEAMS

● ● ● ● ● ● ●

There are deeper sources of resistance, more misconceptions
and tougher obstacles to forming real teams at the top than
at anywhere else in the organization.
—John R. Katzenbach and Douglas K. Smith, *The Wisdom of Teams*

Have you ever worked for an organization that seemed to be moving in many directions at the same time? You felt the volatility as you rebounded between one executive's vision and another, and it was very uncomfortable. This is one of the primary reasons organizations fail. Notwithstanding all their talk about being a team player, valuing collaboration, and making win/win agreements, senior managers have difficulty following their own admonitions. Senior managers have a tendency to be lone rangers. It goes with the territory of leadership. Their individual drive, initiative, and abounding self-confidence dictates that they listen to their own voice. Try as they might, they have difficulty being part of a chorus line.

A few years ago, I was contacted by the managing partner of a law firm with more than two hundred lawyers. The first thing she told me was that the eight members of the executive committee were all headed in different directions. As managing partner, she was having more and more difficulty reaching agreement about things that needed to be decided for the firm's future. Mostly, it wasn't about conflict. No one seemed to care what the others were doing as they went about their own business, doing what they wanted to do. No one was listening to her, and she was running out of energy and patience.

I knew that addressing the situation as one of conflict would not be useful. The lawyers were likely to act in character, by resisting and trying to win. My focus became one of finding the common ground and letting that act as a foundation from which an integrated vision of the future could be established. The only way this tack will work is if you can get everyone away from a "them or me" distributive bargaining perspective (the pie is only so big, so let's fight about how to divide it) and into an integrative bargaining focus (let's look for ways to include other factors or make the pie bigger). I'm happy to report that eight years later the partnership is still going strong. This was the agreement that was worked out.

Agreement

1. Intent and vision: Our joint intention is to be recognized as one of the finest law firms in Chicago. The vision is for a firm that has no difficulty recruiting new associates even though our salary is not the highest. We have the reputation of being a firm that mentors and nurtures new lawyers. Our philosophy is "learning by teaching and doing." High-quality work is our benchmark. We are not concerned with making top-ten lists, only with high quality-of-life ratings. We believe that part of our job as professionals, and officers of the court, is to elevate the quality of the bar and the legal profession. We function in a culture of agreement and resolution, with service to the firm, the firm's culture, society, and the organized bar.

2. Roles: We are the firm's governing body. We seek wisdom and answers from every partner and every associate of the firm. We consider the entire legal services delivery team, which includes the participation of our clients, to be colleagues working together to produce desired client outcomes.

3. *Promises:* Each of us promises:

- To always mentor at least three young lawyers
- To listen to each other
- To become learners
- To become fully engaged in our geographic and other "communities"
- To complete time sheets and have them available as examples
- To attend all management meetings
- To generate at least $50,000 in new billings within the next six months

4. *Time and value:* We work no more than 1400 billable hours and take home at least $200,000.

5. *Measurements of satisfaction:*

- Turnover of less than 30 percent of new associates
- At least an 8-point rating on our self-evaluations
- Twenty-five references to our work in the media by year end

6. *Concerns and fears:*

- That we will shift to an income environment
- That we will forget our agreed core values and become like other firms
- That we will lose our civility
- That in an economic crunch we will not take care of each other
- That we will stop being learners
- That departments will defect

7. Renegotiation: We understand that circumstances change. We view changed circumstances as an opportunity to demonstrate the strength and resiliency of our partnership. We understand that enduring relationships are the key to an ongoing partnership. Only if our relationships survive intact do we have a real partnership.

8. Consequences: If we fail to meet our conditions of satisfaction, we will not be different from other law firms, our personal and firm identity will suffer, and we will loose the value of our vision.

9. Conflict resolution: This shall take place as a triage:
- Talking first
- Informal facilitation by our peers
- Mediation with Stewart Levine
- Resolution with Stewart Levine
- Arbitration with AAA

10. Agreement? Yes! What we have crafted is so much better than not communicating at all.

Summary: Senior managers have a tendency to be lone rangers. It goes with the territory of leadership. Their individual drive, initiative, and self-confidence dictates that they listen to their own voice. Try as they might, they have difficulty being part of a team.

Exercise: If you are a senior manager, ask yourself if you do feel aligned with other members of the senior team. If not, volunteer to facilitate an agreement for results.

CHAPTER 9

AGREEMENTS WITH SUPPLIERS

● ● ● ● ● ● ●

Think of everyone essential to the success of the enterprise as part of it.
Tend toward inclusiveness.
—The Resolutionary

Suppliers are a critical part of all organizations. Your success depends on their delivering what you want for a fair price, on time, and in good condition. Even more than that, it depends on their *anticipating* what your needs will be and fulfilling them. Wouldn't it be great if that was how all supplier relationships were structured? Suppliers as partners, allies, collaborators—part of the team and treated as such. The best example of a supplier as a partner was one I facilitated for a large grocery chain and the company who supplied them with dairy products.

Operating Agreement

1. Intent and vision: It is our intention to create a partnership that is seamless. The vision we have is that all forty-seven of our stores will be supplied with milk and other dairy products in a seamless manner, with little attention needed day to day. The vision is that Metcalf Dairies will monitor dairy products daily,

78

replenish products when needed, and keep freshness levels high while limiting spoilage to between 2 and 4 percent of the gross amount of products delivered.

2. *Roles:* Metcalf will supply the dairy products, and Gengarelli Brothers will supply the store locations. Metcalf will be aware of the times when they need to be out of the supermarket so that inventory can be taken and other products can be delivered.

3. *Promises:* Metcalf promises to (1) deliver the freshest dairy products available, including milk, low-fat milk, half-and-half, yogurt, cottage cheese, and cheese products of all kinds; (2) check and restock inventory daily; (3) keep all display cases full, clean, and free from microbes per the regulations of each county; (4) send drivers who are neat, pleasant, and courteous; and (5) send bills and proof of stocking every fifteen days.

Gengarelli Brothers promises to (1) make adequate shelf space available to Metcalf, (2) pay invoices within twenty days of the date received, (3) conduct biweekly feedback sessions and provide Metcalf with all feedback received.

4. *Time and value:* This agreement will stay in effect until 20 days after it has been canceled by either party, with or without cause. As long as each of us is satisfied with the ongoing quality of the service, we acknowledge the economic and convenience value of the agreement.

5. *Measurements of satisfaction:* The success of our "partnership" will be measured by the following standards:

- Freshness of product: less than 3 precent of milk on shelves at expiration date
- Volume of product sold to be determined on a per-store basis
- Appearance and condition of shelves to be measured by customer surveys

- Compliance with county health regulations
- Less than ten monthly calls for supplemental deliveries

6. Concerns and fears: Metcalf is concerned they we will not get paid in a timely fashion. Gengarelli is concerned that the shelves will not be restocked as promised.

7. Renegotiation: We understand that circumstances change and events will happen that we cannot predict. We agree that if something happens, we will rely on the open communication of our front-line staff first before any management intervention.

8. Consequences: We both recognize the negative consequences of our partnership not working—for Metcalf, the loss of a huge, lucrative account, and for Gengarelli, the need to pay close attention to a department that was essentially self-managed. We also agree that if either one of us breaks a promise, we will donate $100 to the Crossroads Center of Chicago.

9. Conflict resolution: After we have spoken and tried to work out the conflict, the first thing we will do is contact the gentleman who helped us structure this agreement and ask for his help. If that fails, we will bring in a senior management team from both of our organizations. If all else fails, we will use the arbitration services of AAA.

10. Agreement? We are satisfied that we have a clear agreement and the foundation for an ongoing partnership.

This agreement is simple. It structured the relationship in a seamless way and created a context of partnership. It provided the context within which everyone got what they wanted with little direct interaction. This arrangement worked very well for the four-year period before the supplier merged into a larger operation. The beauty of this relationship is that although Metcalf was an independent entity, they functioned as an important part of Gengarelli's business. The Gengarelli management team was relieved of the responsibility for closely managing this important segment of their business.

Summary: Suppliers are a critical part of all organizations. Success depends on their delivering what you want, for a fair price, on time, and in good condition. It is important to see suppliers as partners, allies, and collaborators who are part of the team and recognized as such.

Exercise: Can you think of a supplier to your organization who could be a real partner, like the example in the chapter? See if the supplier is interested in speculating about how that would serve both of you. Use the template to structure an agreement.

CHAPTER 10

SALES AGREEMENTS

● ● ● ● ● ● ●

Market to the elite and eat with the masses.
But market to the masses and eat with the elite.
—Unknown

Once the sale is closed, it's time to create a document that expresses the agreement between the people or organizations involved. This should be a simple process of writing down what was sold, what was bought, and the terms on which it will be delivered. Wouldn't it be great if the agreement captured the good feelings that surround a new relationship. That was the basis for consummation of the transaction. Unfortunately, often the opposite happens.

In many situations, the "seller" delivers a form contract that details what was bought and what was sold, and the back of the form is filled with miniscule boilerplate legal jargon. The agreement does not reflect the relationship that developed in the sales process. Instead of solidifying the relationship, the agreement can drive a wedge between people that darkens the "blush" they were experiencing when they "shook hands." The document should reflect more than the business and legal requirements. It should embody the spirit of the agreement, reflecting the relationship created and everyone's positive vision and expectation.

I am often disappointed when I trust someone else to do the sales agreement. I am disappointed because the agreement does little to make me feel comfortable or manage my expectations effectively. How do you respond when presented with the following clauses taken from a standard agreement to purchase a new car? This was the agreement my father was presented.

Standard Auto Sales Agreement Clauses

On the front, in standard type size:

1. AS IS—WITH ALL FAULTS. The only warranties applying to this vehicle are those offered by the Manufacturer and the applicability of any existing Manufacturer's warranty, if any, shall be determined solely by such Manufacturer's warranty. The selling dealer hereby expressly disclaims all warranties, either expressed or implied, including any implied warranties of merchantability or fitness for a particular purpose, and neither assumes nor authorizes any person to assume for it any liability in connection with the sale of this vehicle. Buyer shall not be entitled to recover from the selling dealer for any consequential damages, damages to property, damages for loss of use, loss of time, loss of profits, or income, or any other incidental damages. The Purchaser hereby acknowledges that Seller has made available "Warranty Pre-Sale Information" as disclosed in the Warranty Binders pursuant to the Magnuson-Moss Warranty Act.

2. ANY CONTROVERSY OR CLAIM ARISING OUT OF OR RELATING TO THIS CONTRACT, OR BREACH THEREOF, SHALL BE SETTLED BY ARBITRATION IN THE COUNTY IN WHICH THE CAR WAS SOLD IN ACCORDANCE WITH THE RULES OF THE AMERICAN ARBITRATION ASSOCIATION AND JUDGEMENT UPON THE AWARD RENDERED BY THE ARBITRATOR(S) MAY BE ENTERED IN ANY COURT HAVING JURISDICTION THEREOF.

On the back, in tiny type:

2. Manufacturer has reserved the right to change the price to Dealer of new motor vehicles without notice. In the event the price to Dealer of new motor vehicles of the series and body type ordered hereunder is changed by Manufacturer prior to delivery of the new motor vehicle ordered hereunder to Buyer, Dealer reserves the right to change the cash delivered price of such motor vehicle to Buyer accordingly. If such cash delivered price is increased by Dealer, Buyer may, if dissatisfied therewith, cancel this Order, in which event if a used motor vehicle has been traded in as part of the consideration for such new motor vehicle, such used motor vehicle shall be returned to Buyer upon payment of a reasonable charge for storage and repairs (if any) or, if such used motor vehicle has been previously sold by dealer, the amount received therefore less a selling commission of 15% and any expense incurred in storing, insuring, conditioning or advertising said used motor vehicle for sale shall be returned to Buyer.

4. Buyer agrees to deliver to Dealer satisfactory evidence of title to any used motor vehicle traded in as part of the consideration for the motor vehicle ordered hereunder at the time of delivery of such used motor vehicle to Dealer. Buyer warrants any such used motor vehicle to be his property, free and clear of all liens and encumbrances except otherwise noted herein. Buyer agrees that any undisclosed existing liens on the vehicle traded in will be the sole responsibility of Buyer and that he will cause to be satisfied such lien or liens within 72 hours of Dealer's notice in writing and that upon your failure to make such lien satisfaction, the dealer shall have the right to repossession of the newly purchased car, without legal action, and this agreement shall become null and void and without effect, except that dealer shall be entitled to any moneys and/or trade in as liquidated damages, the amount thereof not to exceed the sum expended by Dealer in furtherance of the consummation of this transaction (for example, paying off existing acknowledged indebtedness on trade-ins) plus ten percent (10%) of purchase price.

5. When fully executed by both parties, unless this order shall have been canceled by Buyer under and in accordance with the provisions of paragraph 2 or 3 above, Dealer shall have the right, upon failure or refusal of Buyer to accept delivery, within 10 days of the motor vehicle ordered hereunder and to comply with the terms of this order, to retain as liquidated damages any partial payment made by Buyer, and in the event a used motor vehicle has been traded in as part of the consideration for the motor vehicle ordered hereunder, to sell such used motor vehicle and reimburse himself out of the proceeds of such sale for the expenses specified in paragraph 2 above and for such other expenses and losses as Dealer may incur or suffer as a result of such failure or refusal by Buyer, including, but not limited to, storage charges of $10 per day.

6. Manufacturer has reserved the right to change the design of any new motor vehicle, chassis, accessories, or parts thereof at any time without notice and without obligation to make the same or any similar change upon any motor vehicle, chassis, accessories, or parts thereof previously purchased or shipped to Dealer or being manufactured or sold in accordance with Dealer's orders. Correspondingly, in the event of any such change by manufacturer, Dealer shall have no obligation to Buyer to make the same or any similar change in any motor vehicle, chassis, or accessories or parts thereof covered by this order either before or subsequent to delivery thereof to Buyer.

11. The Dealer does not warrant or in any way guarantee the mileage indicated on this vehicle's odometer to be

accurate, correct, or that it may not have been so changed
or adjusted by owners or persons in possession prior to the
Dealer.

17. THE DEALER MAKES NO WARRANTIES, EXPRESS OR IMPLIED,
INCLUDING ANY IMPLIED WARRANTY OF MERCHANTABILITY OR
FITNESS OF A PARTICULAR PURPOSE, WITH RESPECT TO THE
VEHICLE OR CHASSIS DESCRIBED ON THE FACE HEREOF, EXCEPT
AS MAY BE OTHERWISE SPECIFICALLY PROVIDED IN WRITING ON
THE FACE OF THIS ORDER OR IN A SEPARATE WRITING FUR-
NISHED TO BUYER TO DEALER. IN THE CASE OF A NEW VEHICLE
OR CHASSIS, AT THE TIME OF DELIVERY, DEALER SHALL DELIVER
TO BUYER THE MANUFACTURER'S PRINTED NEW VEHICLE WAR-
RANTY WITH RESPECT TO SUCH NEW VEHICLE OR CHASSIS. IN
THE CASE OF A USED VEHICLE OR CHASSIS, THE APPLICABILITY
THERETO OF THE EXISTING MANUFACTURER'S WARRANTY, IF
ANY, SHOULD BE DETERMINED SOLELY FROM THE TERMS OF
SUCH WARRANTY. ALL WARRANTIES, IF ANY, BY A MANUFAC-
TURER OR SUPPLIER OTHER THAN THE DEALER ARE THEIRS,
NOT DEALERS. AND ONLY SUCH MANUFACTURER OR OTHER
SUPPLIER SHALL BE LIABLE FOR PERFORMANCE UNDER SUCH
WARRANTIES.

18. The buyer hereby agrees that if it becomes necessary for
Dealer to enforce or defend any of its rights or remedies
under this Buyer's Order, Dealer shall be entitled to recover
from the Buyer all costs and reasonable attorney's fees,
including such costs and fees for any appeals. This agreement shall be construed and interpreted in accordance
with the laws of the State of Florida. Buyer waives trial by
jury and further consents to venue of any processing or
lawsuit being in Broward County, Florida.

Here is something that looks and feels a lot different.

We Pledge to You

1. Intent and vision: The intention is for you, the buyer, to have a joyful experience, both driving your new vehicle and working with Diamond Motors to keep you and the vehicle "satisfied" at all times. The vision we have is that all aspects of the sales and service experience will be positive for you: picking up the vehicle, bringing the vehicle in for warranty work, and bringing the vehicle in for repairs.

2. Roles: We will be the expert service provider and caregiver. You will be the satisfied customer.

3. Promises: We will treat you as we would treat a guest in our home. We promise to be pleasant and courteous at all times, to provide a loaner car when the need for service is due to a defect in the car or our service, or because you must have one. We promise to find out what your personal expectations are and satisfy them. We will take care of you and the vehicle. We promise to repair the vehicle within the time and cost estimate promised. You promise to tell us what needs attention and to make payment on time.

4. Time and value: This agreement remains in place for the life of the vehicle. We agree that we are satisfied with our return for the transaction. We want you always to feel the transaction was worthwhile.

5. Measurements of satisfaction: You give us a 4.5 or better on our survey every time your car is in for service.

6. Concerns and fears: You indicated that you fear that once the agreement is signed, you will become just another automobile buyer. We promise to do everything we can to make your fears go away. Our fear is that you expect perfection.

7. *Renegotiation:* We will negotiate every aspect of our purchase agreement that is not required by law.

8. *Consequences:* If we lose you as a customer, we lose you for life, and that represents an average revenue stream of $175,000. If our service is not done on time and to your satisfaction, we will not charge you for the repairs.

9. *Conflict resolution:* We will have our designated customer service representative speak with you. If that does not work, we will use the mediation services of our local Better Business Bureau, and if that fails to produce resolution, we will use the arbitration services of AAA.

10. *Agreement?* We hope you are satisfied with our agreement.

Of the two agreements presented, which one do you prefer? Which one engenders more trust and willingness to be in a long-term business relationship? I have presented these contrasting agreements to illustrate what the accepted common practice is and what our aspirational model looks like. As with many situations, the extremes don't really serve the situation fully. A combination of protection and results may be best for certain situations. The points to take away are that *you always have choice* and that it is important to realize the long-term effect of the agreement you propose and the agreement you accept.

Summary: A written agreement (artifact) describing what someone has purchased might contain much more than the business and legal requirements. It can embody the spirit of the agreement, reflecting the relationship created, as well as the positive vision and expectation everyone has for the present time and for the future.

Exercise: If you have recently sold or purchased any high-ticket consumer goods, please notice if the sales agreement is filled with clauses like the ones from the auto sales agreement. How do you respond to those clauses? Do you read them? What clauses might you put in a sales agreement? How might those clauses improve the relationship with a buyer?

CHAPTER 11

TEAM AGREEMENTS

● ● ● ● ● ● ●

Because the WaWa, the Canada Goose, flies in formation, it is freedom
tempered by responsibility. The leader must keep the group on course and look
ahead for danger. The others must look around, to the sides, to each other.
And they will reach their destination, not because they can fly, but because
they fly together. We too, seek to fly. To fulfill our dreams, to accomplish our
goals. But we cannot fly alone. We must always look ahead, behind, and to
the welfare of those who seek to fly with us. If our destination is a better way
of life we must demonstrate our commitment to work with one another.
If we are to fly, we must fly together, dependent on each other, or
be scattered by the storms that confront us.
—WaWa Corporation Philosophy

A few years ago, at the height of popularity of Self-Directed Work Teams, I was working with a government agency to implement a team environment for a unit of technical support people. The challenge was not only to create "teams" but also to bring out the entrepreneurial spirit in each member of the organization.

The critical part of a successful team environment is making sure everyone has the same vision before moving into action. The classic "forming, storming, norming, performing" stages that teams traverse are best resolved with an agreement. The agreement serves the "norming" function as members of the team agree on how they will work with one another, what their norms will be. The agreement reflects the resolution of their "storming." With some coaching help, the following agreement was put in place to govern team activities.

Team Agreement

1. *Intent and vision:* All members of "The Programmers" agree to follow the terms of this agreement. Our vision is to be a tightly coordinated unit whose members are cross-trained in the jobs of all members of the team so that any one of us could step into a client request at any moment. The specific vision we have is that we will be self-supporting within two years; we will generate enough revenue to cover our costs and our salaries. We will:

- Train each other in what we do
- Become competent salespeople
- Sell our core competencies to other government and nongovernment agencies
- Become a role model for what an entrapreneurial government agency can do
- Become qualified experts in providing programming support for the growing technology business community;
- Pool our resources so that some of us will become salespeople while others will be engaged in direct, immediate, revenue opportunities.

2. *Roles:* We will each become entrepreneurs, life-long learners, teammates, and a "work family" who realize we are each essential to the others' survival during a time of government and military downsizing. We realize a cooperative management team and a steady stream of new, solvent clients is critical to our success.

3. Promises: We each promise to accept rewards on a team basis only, to give each other ongoing honest feedback on matters that impact our work and productivity, to accept that we are beginners in the realm of interpersonal communication, to devote our full time energy to the work of the team, to teach teammates what we learn when we take a training class, to come to team meetings on time, to follow the standards for team meetings we have drafted, to stay in a learning mode, and to take our turn as team leader.

4. Time and value: We each agree that the potential benefits of being a team far outweigh the costs involved, and we agree to experiment with the team method of organizing work for the next two years.

5. Measurements of satisfaction: Our measure of success will be sustainability—how long it takes to become self-sustaining. We have set a goal of eighteen months to become self-supporting, to make revenue equal expenses plus salaries.

6. Concerns and fears: We are concerned that in six months a new management fad will be put in place or that we will be reassigned to other units and our operation will be completely shut down. We are also concerned that members of the team will leave for other departments or nongovernment jobs.

7. Renegotiation: We understand the importance of ongoing communication. In that spirit, we see our team agreement as a living, evolving context in which we work together. We agree to keep our agreement current; we will look at it monthly to make sure it reflects the reality of what we are doing as a unit. We see "teamship" as a voluntary activity and agree that if anyone wants to leave the team, they can.

8. Consequences: We assume that all of us combined are smarter than any one of us. We agree to defer to the team to determine consequences for any violation of this team agreement. We realize that when we violate an expressed or implied responsibility of teamship, a consequence should follow. We fully understand that if we are not successful at becoming self-sustaining, our unit may be disbanded and we will be left without jobs.

9. *Conflict resolution:* We agree to the following rules: (1) manage your own emotions; (2) talk to the person or group you are in conflict with; (3) ask a team member to mediate; (4) get the entire team involved; (5) ask the team coach for help.

10. *Agreement?* We are confident that all of us together are stronger than if we worked independently during this time of change and transition. We all take responsibility for managing the team as we rotate team leadership.

Team members reported that they enjoyed the process and found that the dialogue generated closer relationships and that they use their agreement as a way of orienting new team members. The agreement has become a combination operations and personnel manual for the team.

Summary: The critical part of a successful team environment is making sure everyone has the same vision before moving into action. The classic "forming, storming, norming, performing" stages that teams traverse is best resolved with an agreement. The agreement serves the norming function as members of the team agree on how they will work with each other, what their norms will be. The agreement reflects the resolution of their "storming."

Exercise: What teams are you part of at work and within your community? Select a team that you are part of and prepare a team agreement.

CHAPTER 12

DIVERSITY AGREEMENTS

● ● ● ● ● ● ●

After the first few months of deadly trench warfare during World War I,
Christmas Day, 1914, dawned bright and cold, freezing the sea of mud
between the enemies. Allied and Axis soldiers spilled out of the trenches and
spontaneously gathered in the middle of No-Man's-Land, exchanging gifts,
playing soccer, and rediscovering their common humanity. Reacting in horror
at the implications of such behavior, the generals forbade further fraterniza-
tion under the threat of death. And so the war continued. But for one moment
in the midst of all that anger, hatred, and violence a new force emerged. A
strange attractor—love—took over and transformed reality.
—David La Chapelle, *Navigating the Tides of Change*

What happened on the front line demonstrates what is possible when we can get beyond the parochial ways we have been taught and grow into the inclusiveness that is innately present in each one of us. Until recently, for many organizations, diversity programs were about compliance with either a legal or organizational mandate. That has changed dramatically. Diversity is now about viability in a diverse world. Failing to become a diverse organization is a huge strategic blunder. A lack of diversity inhibits an organization from being effective in both the domestic and global marketplace.

If you do not have a diverse perspective, you will find it

increasingly difficult to design products and services that will appeal to a diverse global marketplace. The perspective of all groups will be missing from the mix, so the design will likely have a large gap. I think it would be very difficult for a large city department store to succeed without African, Asian, Latin, and Anglo Americans on the team. Simply put, it's bad business strategy.

If I were in charge of an organization I would make everyone conscious of the strategic value of diversity by having everyone sign a pledge like the following:

Diversity Pledge

*1. **Intent and vision:*** It is the intent of the Alexis organization, and every one of its employees, to honor the reality that it is sound business to have an organizational culture that is multiethnic and multiracial.

*2. **Roles:*** Alexis agrees to foster a diverse environment by making sure that diversity is not an issue for any of the operational units under its control. Every employee of Alexis agrees to become a champion of diversity because it contributes to the business results of the organization. Alexis promises to be thorough in all of its recruiting.

*3. **Promises:*** Promise is a loaded word! Some thrive on making and fulfilling promises. Their identity is entwined with the promises they make and keep. Every member of Alexis promises to:

- Personally take on the responsibility for consciously learning how to thrive in a multiracial world by making it part of their learning plan
- Comply with developing standards that determine if an organization has a global culture
- Seek diverse perspectives when making major business decisions

4. Time and value: We have no question that we will derive benefit far greater than the small investment in human capital.

5. Measurements of satisfaction: We want Alexis to reflect America's population demographics. We will measure our level of diversity by the following standards: We will strive to include the following population groups in our organization in the same proportion as they are in the U.S. population within two years.

- African American
- Anglo American
- Asian American
- Disabled Americans
- Gay and Lesbian Americans
- Latin American
- Middle-Eastern American
- Senior Americans
- Young Americans

6. Concerns and fears: We are all concerned about our ability to make this vision a reality. The fear we have is that people will feel strange and self-conscious about working with other ethnic groups. We understand that learning to work effectively within a multiracial and multiethnic organization is of great value to us collectively, individually, and in our personal lives.

7. Renegotiation: We acknowledge that global concerns are shifting rapidly. As time changes and we know more about the global marketplace, we agree to revisit the question of what it means to be a diverse culture and how to achieve it. Having said that, we are certain that what will not change is the common humanity everyone shares.

8. Consequences: We feel so strongly about diversity, as both a value and a success strategy, that we agree that if anyone fails to honor our diversity standards, after appropriate notice and a chance to move toward compliance, they will be terminated, and they will forfeit their rights to any severance benefits.

9. Conflict resolution: If anyone has conflicts related to diversity concerns, they agree to a mediation process facilitated by a member of the offended minority group.

10. Agreement? YES! We believe we have a meeting of the minds, and that we have recognized a critical business need.

Summary: Not becoming a diverse organization is a huge strategic mistake. It inhibits an organization from being effective in both the domestic and global marketplace. If you do not have a diverse perspective, you will likely find it difficult to design products and services that will appeal to a diverse global marketplace.

Exercise: Look around your organization. Do you consider it to be a diverse organization? Why? How does it measure up against other organizations in the same arena? Is being part of the organization teaching you something about working in a diverse environment? Has your organization moved from valuing diversity to behaving as if it does?

CHAPTER 13

LEARNING AGREEMENTS

● ● ● ● ● ● ●

I have learnt silence from the talkative, toleration from the intolerant, and
kindness from the unkind; yet strange, I am ungrateful to these teachers.
—Kahlil Gibran

The term *learning organization* was first popularized by Peter Senge in his 1990 classic *The Fifth Discipline.*[5] His thesis was that our culture had become so complex, and the organizational pressure for creativity and innovation had become so great, that the only way organizations and individuals could possibly succeed in the face of immense challenges was to band together in "learning organizations," populated by "learners," who would "learn" their way through to the solutions of problems. Senge, it seems, was picking up on what Albert Einstein said about the need to "invent new ideas to deal with the current challenges."

In the mid 1990s, I was called by a high-tech company for assistance with its learning challenges. This company existed in a very competitive environment. Although its managers were familiar with Senge's work, it had not embraced the ideas as a cornerstone of its culture. The company never realized that a benefit of fostering a learning environment is the high level of productivity individuals experience when they are learning. There is a physiological reaction in the body to learning. Much as in distance running, when we are learning, endorphins are released that contribute to a sense of euphoria.

After working at a number of levels within the organization, I thought the best way to get them beyond where they were stuck was not to process what they reported as ongoing conflicts but to shift their entire operating paradigm to that of the learning organization. Because many of the executive and senior staff were "ex pat" academics, it was not difficult to get them to embrace this idea. They quickly understood why I had reframed conflict resolution as a "learning exercise" where each participant in a conflict, rather than trying to win, acts like a teacher, educating everyone else about their point of view, needs, and concerns.

I wanted to get buy-in from all levels of the company. First I worked with the senior executive team and their staff. Then I brought what they articulated, along with some of the team, to teach what they had created through learning. The product of that conference was then brought to the operational level of the organization. This is the agreement they worked out.

Learning Agreement

1. Intent and vision: Our intention is to become a learning organization filled with individual learners. Because all of us together are smarter than any one of us alone, we have come to recognize that the only way we can stay successful and competitive is to learn from and to teach each other. We believe this is the key to long-term success as an organization. Vicariously, each individual will have the knowledge that he or she was a contribution to a collaborative team of learners. Our vision is that our scientists, who previously worked alone, will collaborate more. We also believe that getting sales, R&D, and manufacturing to learn and to teach each other will make our organization healthy. Our bottom-line goal is to get people in the company to think beyond their own territoriality, to share, and to respect what others have to contribute. Our hope is that becoming a learning organization will empower others because they will feel listened to and heard.

2. *Role:* We will all be teachers, learners, facilitators of information, and knowledge transferers. We will come to meetings with a mindset that is inclusive and considers things from an enterprise, not a departmental perspective. We will come as resources for others.

3. *Promises:* We each promise to:

- Listen and learn from what is being said
- Allow ourselves to be impacted by what others have to say
- Let go of any notion that inside an organization it is appropriate to play a right/wrong, win/lose; or blame/fault game
- See all others inside the organization as part of the same team doing their best to feel proud of the products and services we offer, enjoy our workplace relationships, and to earn a decent living
- Be vigilant about the need to exchange ideas and collaborate effectively
- Look for the contribution others make because of their unique genius

4. *Time and value:* This agreement will remain in effect until we design a better framework for organizational health and effectiveness. We believe the potential personal and professional rewards will more than compensate for the time we invest in embracing a new cultural mantra.

5. *Measurements of satisfaction:* We agree to measure the value of our "learning organization" by (a) bottom line financial results, (b) creative results in terms of new/improved product designs, and (c) relationship/interpersonal results as measured by agreed upon observable standards.

6. *Concerns and fears:* We are concerned that individuals will not be able to fully embrace this new culture because of personal habits and the pervasive organizational culture of competition. We fear that the way in which we are evaluated will not be changed by management and that traditional formal management measurement will pull in the opposite direction than the direction we are headed. We fear that this will be just another failed "management intervention of the month"—a failure that will leave us more disillusioned than ever.

7. *Renegotiation:* This agreement is eminently renegotiable because of our belief that the ongoing relationships and learning that takes place between people can become dominant, and that is much more important than the details of this agreement.

8. *Consequences:* We fully understand the potential consequences of this agreement not working. Potential negative consequences include bankruptcy of the company and loss of jobs, salaries, stock options, and friendships.

9. *Conflict resolution:* We agree to use the methods and models found in *Getting to Resolution.*

10. *Agreement?* We believe we have created the foundation on which all levels of the organization are engaged in shifting our culture.

About a year after the agreement was crafted, I met with the senior executives of the organization. They told me that the agreement we crafted, somewhat to their surprise and delight, had a profound impact on their organizational health and productivity.

They reported that the culture became more collegial, that ideas and information flowed, and that the environment shifted from a solo mentality to one in which everyone was under the same tent.

Summary: The only way organizations and individuals can possibly succeed in the face of immense challenges is to band together in "learning organizations," populated by individuals who can "learn" their way through to the solutions of problems that do not have current answers.

Exercise: What are you learning at work? Do you think you are part of a learning organization? Do you face challenges that need the help of others? What are you currently doing about it? What could you do about it?

CHAPTER 14

JOINT VENTURE AGREEMENTS

● ● ● ● ● ● ●

Pioneers are motivated by drive to achievement and by irrational optimism
rather than by reasonable calculation. If those who start a business rely on
nothing but mathematical expectation enterprise will fade and die.

—John Maynard Keynes

A joint venture is an agreement between two or more organizations who undertake a project together. As the world becomes more virtual, the need for what "strategic partners" can bring to joint ventures will become more pervasive. The good news lies in the possibility of achieving the best of all worlds by being able to put great teams together for specific projects without taking on additional staff. The challenges lie in quick integration, coordination, and control. People starting a joint venture often posture for protection. Unfortunately, as you are aware by now, posturing takes the focus off the vision of results that generated the initial excitement and optimism about the project.

I recently was part of a team organizing a joint venture between the Law Practice Management Section of the American Bar Association (LPM) and a private conference promoter, Legal Management (LM), to sponsor a law-firm management educational conference. Here's the joint venture agreement I crafted.

Law Firm Management Institute

1. Intent and vision: Our intention is to produce an educational conference called the Law Firm Management Institute in the fall of 2002. Our vision for the conference is that it will be modeled after the success and growth of LPM TechShow. We want it to become the place where people come to gather leading-edge information that will help them deliver legal services in the most profitable and efficient way. In the first year, it will be a single-track, two-day conference targeted at people with management responsibility—managing partners, general counsel, practice group leaders, administrators, and senior managers. As the conference becomes more successful, it will be expanded to three days with additional tracks for corporate law departments, government law offices, small firms, and solos.

2. Roles: LPM will be primarily responsible for content design and securing speakers. LPM will also add its identity and logo. LM will be responsible for financing, organization, and administration as more specifically defined by the promises that follow.

3. Promises:
LM promises to take care of:
- Planning—appoint and chair planning committee to work with LPM speakers—selection, schedule, accommodations
- Brochure—drafting, review and approval, printing, securing mailing lists
- Mailing
- Program development—workshop sessions and agenda
- Program materials—supply books, prepare evaluations, develop handouts
- Facilities—site selection, reservations, beverages for breaks, food service

- Registration
- Special equipment—VCR, cabling, monitors, overhead projector, LCD, easels, markers
- Registrations—receive and process, receive and account for, prepare list, staff table, apply and administer CLE credit
- Miscellaneous—local publicity, program moderators, compile evaluation forms
- Financial—80 percent profit-sharing after expenses, prepare projected budget, prepare final accounting. LM will be solely responsible for all expenses and LPM will have no liability for expenses. All direct out-of-pocket expenses associated with the program will be paid by LM, including travel, meal, and hotel expenses of speakers and LPM and LM staff who travel to the program site, paid in accordance with LM reimbursement policies and procedures.

LPM promises to take care of:
- Planning—appoint and chair planning committee to work with GLW
- Speakers—selection
- Brochure—review and approval
- Program development—workshop sessions and agenda
- Program materials—develop handouts
- Logo—with prior approval, enable LM to use its name and logo on promotional and program material
- Miscellaneous—cooperate with national and local publicity, program moderators
- Financial—20 percent profit-sharing after expenses

4. Time and value: We each agree that if this conference is as well attended and as content-rich as we envision, we will continue staging it from year to year. We also acknowledge that if the conference is successful, we will be satisfied with the financial and other value generated by our effort.

5. *Measurements of satisfaction:* We will consider this program successful in the first year if we have 200 paying attendees, generate $50,000 after expenses, receive average evaluations of 4.5 points on a 5-point scale, and decide to repeat and expand the conference next year.

6. *Concerns and fears:* That attendance will be low; that the quality of speakers and programs will be less than outstanding; that it will not be profitable.

7. *Renegotiation:* Given that this is the first year of this joint venture, we anticipate a great deal of renegotiation because we have not done this before.

8. *Consequences:* Both parties' pride will be hurt if the conference is not successful.

9. *Conflict resolution:* We will continue to talk until we need to find a mediator to help us.

10. *Agreement?* Yes, we look forward to working with each other.

Given the context, it is amazing to note the lack of legalese and protective language. For me, this is very telling. At a place more profound than their professional skills, lawyers understand that working well together is about trust and collaboration. You would be surprised at how many law-firm partnerships do not have written agreements.

Summary: A joint venture is an agreement between two or more organizations who undertake a project together. Often people starting a joint venture posture for protection. That takes the focus off the vision of results that initially generated excitement and optimism about the project.

Exercise: Are you facing a challenge for which you don't have the knowledge and experience? Is their a person or organization that does have what you need? Have you considered asking them to participate in a joint venture? If you can identify a potential partner, use the agreement to structure a dialogue to discover if a joint venture is appropriate.

CHAPTER 15

AGREEMENTS BETWEEN DEPARTMENTS

● ● ● ● ● ● ●

*There is no single correct way of approaching complex systems and their
interactions in the world, though the art of listening is a most desirable skill.
. . . Multiple realities inform each other, fertilize, stimulate,
and stir the cauldron of creativity.*
—David La Chapelle, *Navigating the Tides of Change*

One of the most significant ingredients for effective and efficient
organizational productivity is the ability of departments to collaborate effectively. Although it should be obvious to all concerned,
people often "forget" that everyone is engaged in the same mission. Unfortunately, the norm is for turf battles and department-centric behavior to develop. More times than I care to recall I have
facilitated dialogue among sales, manufacturing, and implementation. The problem is almost always a lack of communication coupled with a perception of "us/them" in the other department. Here
is a representative example of one of the "fixes" I facilitated for a
major telecommunications organization. It is critical to keep
reminding everyone that they are all inside the same circle.

Collaboration Agreement

1. Intent and vision: It is our intention to have effective coordination among sales, manufacturing, and installation. Our vision

108

for the future is one of close coordination among our departments, with no one making promises or representations until they have confirmed the accuracy and ability to deliver with all three departments. We want to accomplish this with the pre-sales visit and the pre-contract and pre- and post-installation meetings. Our goal is to eliminate the conflicts that always develop.

2. *Roles:* Everyone plays an essential part in the process. Manufacturing is responsible for building what the customer orders after it has been designed by the installation and sales team, who coordinate with any technical departments. The sales role is that of customer advocate. The salesperson's primary role is communication and coordination. The entire organization depends on sales to find, service, and please customers by making them satisfied with what we have to offer. The installation team is responsible to make sure what was ordered is delivered and installed and that the customer is satisfied that their needs are being taken care of.

3. *Promises:*

Sales promises to:

- Sell only what we can manufacture
- Become very familiar with our products as described in our brochures and technical specs
- Check with production and installation schedules before making any promises to the customer
- Stop holding manufacturing and installation as adversaries and start thinking of them as resources who will be helpful in our jobs
- Honor our organizational pricing guidelines when submitting quotes
- Stop saying negative things about manufacturing and installation
- Let go of the perception that manufacturing and installation are a bunch of "engineering bureaucrats"

Manufacturing promises to:

- Cooperate at all times with sales on both delivery times and customization, especially when needed to close the sale
- Move away from the immediate reaction of "no" when a request comes from sales about a prospective new order
- Use our creativity to look for ways of accommodating the customer
- Recognize that sales and installation stand on the same footing and are just as important to the success of the organization as manufacturing

Installation promises to:

- Restrain ourselves from making negative comments about sales and manufacturing when we are installing a system
- Embrace sales and manufacturing as real teammates
- Recognize that without sales and manufacturing, we would not have a job

4. Time and value: We all understand and acknowledge that we are interdependent and that without each other we would not have a viable organization. We recognize that the role each of us plays is an essential part of satisfying the customer. There is no question of the value that will come back to us if we honor the terms of this agreement. For that reason, we will continue to honor the terms of this agreement for as long as we are in business.

5. Measurements of satisfaction: We will measure our success in keeping our promises under this agreement by the following standards: how often we raise our voices; how many times customers call our senior executives with complaints; how many testimonials we get from customers; how many missed on-time deliveries we have each quarter; our respective levels of stress and

anxiety; who our emotions are directed at; our ability to acknowledge and enjoy our colleagues from other departments.

6. *Concerns and fears:* We are all concerned that the stereotyp-
ing and resentments have built up over such a long time that we
will not be able to get beyond them. We are also concerned that no
one will change their behavior, that sales will make whatever
promises necessary to close a deal, that manufacturing will resist
anything that is inconvenient, and that installation will not take
ownership of projects and service the customer properly.

7. *Renegotiations:* We all acknowledge that opening this dialogue has already resulted in easing the tension. We are getting
beyond classifying one another as "the enemy." It looks as if, much
to our surprise, we are developing a collaborative relationship. We
trust that as we discover more about how the other departments
operate, we will be able to refine our working relationship. We
understand that how we work together and serve the customer is
much more important than the words of this agreement.

8. *Consequences:* We realize that failing to honor this agreement
is a potential disaster for the customer and for each of us. We agree
that when either one of us breaks a promise under this agreement,
we will deposit $5 in our charity fund.

9. *Conflict resolution:* If conflict develops between us that
we cannot resolve within two days, we agree to ask our VP of
operations to help us mediate the situation. If we can't agree, he
can make a decision for us. We will honor that decision without
resentment.

10. *Agreement?* We are satisfied and looking forward to working
with one another.

When I reflect on the need for this kind of agreement it informs me that as a culture we are doing something wrong, both with the educational models and cultural norms we are instilling in neophyte minds and with people who might have learned differently and "should" know better. I do think we *know* that collaboration is a higher form of human interaction, and when a safe context is provided, we can jump right in. We also understand that in certain contexts, competition brings out the best in us. What seems to be missing is the wisdom to make discerning choices about the best "driver" for particular situations. Making those kind of judgments is the kind of education we need as a collective. That seems more important than instilling an omnipresent sense of "winning" at any cost. What we need are new contextual definitions of victory!

Summary: One of the most significant impediments to effective and efficient organizational productivity is the ability of departments to collaborate effectively. Unfortunately, the norm is often turf battles and department-centric behavior. The cause is almost always a lack of communication coupled with a perception of "us/them" in the other department.

Exercise: Do you engage in "us/them" thinking when reflecting on your relationship with other departments of your organization? Are they really the enemy? Do you think a dialogue with "them" would be useful?

CHAPTER 16

PERFORMANCE APPRAISAL
AGREEMENTS

● ● ● ● ● ● ●

Performance appraisal does not and cannot work. It's a new century now.
It's time to start over now and look for new ways to liberate
the human spirit in organizational life.
—Tom Coens and Mary Jenkins, *Abolishing Performance Appraisals*

Everyone endures them in some form or another. And everybody hates them! I have no doubt that when reporting relationships are working well, appraisals are no surprise—merely a summary of what everyone already knows. They are more for other people than for those directly involved. I think the primary reason appraisals are not productive is because they play into people's aversion to authority and the perceived underlying power imbalances. Once power comes into play, conflict becomes part of the milieu.

The following agreement was put in place to deal with this dreaded monster after performance appraisals surfaced as one of the areas of conflict within a government agency. When I suggested that an ongoing, authentic, open dialogue would go a long way to alleviating rampant "appraisal-itis," everyone laughed, but they knew we had touched a truth.

Curing the Appraisal "Virus"

1. Intent and vision: It is our intention to eliminate the tension and apprehension surrounding performance appraisals. Our vision for the future is that the formal appraisal will be nothing more than a report containing a summary of the ongoing dialogue that has been taking place.

2. Roles: The supervisor will be the person giving constructive feedback. The people reporting to them will be the learner. The purpose of the feedback will be for learning and growth.

3. Promises: The supervisor promises to provide ongoing feedback as necessary. The feedback will be instructional, for the purposes of learning and continual improvement. The supervisor promises to make the feedback about behavior and to provide specific suggestions about how the outcome could be improved. Part of the feedback will be devoted to grooming the learner to take over the supervisor's position. The learner agrees not to take the feedback personally and to acknowledge that it is not to be about right or wrong but about learning, improvement, and how people can work together more effectively. The supervisor agrees that performance appraisals will not contain any surprises. The feedback will be an ongoing process of bridge building that is part of a learning environment of continual improvement.

4. Time and value: We all agree that the huge relief of not having to participate in the fear-based context of appraisals is of great value. We agree that the potential of learning is much more valuable than the time it will require weekly. We have no difficulty devoting the time to make it work.

5. Measurements of satisfaction: Learning that results in qualitative improvement in job competence, and no surprises.

6. *Concerns and fears:* That we won't take the time to do the ongoing work of learning for continual improvement; that supervisors will feel compelled to operate on a bell-curve model where they are obligated to find things "wrong" and to give people "demerits."

7. *Renegotiation:* This is an experiment. We realize that by continuing to fine-tune as we learn by experience, we will improve our results and our relationships.

8. *Consequences:* A return to anxiety-filled apprehension about periodic and annual performance reviews. Individuals, and thus the organization, will be forced once more to go through this ritual. Remembering the current environment will motivate us to succeed with our experiment.

9. *Conflict resolution:* We recognize that there is great potential for conflict in appraisal situations and that people may still get defensive and take things personally. We agree to have cooling-off periods and then to set aside the time for a resolution process. We agree to use the Levine Seven-Step Model. If we can't get to agreement ourselves, we agree that another member of the team will facilitate.

10. *Agreement?* We feel great about this opportunity.

The open dialogue that was the basis for the agreement was much more important than the document. Talking about the place in the system that was blocking a free flow of creative energy opened many new possibilities for higher levels of productivity. Once the fear was lifted of being judged on a win/lose scale, everyone could relax into working for results instead of working in the fear of a "losing" evaluation.

Summary: No one likes the ritual of formal performance appraisals. The formal appraisal should be nothing more than a report containing a summary of ongoing dialogue that has been taking place. Articulating this as an agreement and practice alleviates a great deal of the anxiety surrounding this sometimes-barbaric ritual.

Exercise: Have a discussion with your boss and all the people who report to you about performance appraisals. Suggest that you would like to put your thoughts into a short agreement. Prepare an agreement like the template in this chapter.

CHAPTER 17

FEEDBACK AGREEMENTS

● ● ● ● ● ● ●

Skillful feedback is the best source about how our behavior is impacting oth-
ers. Taking it seriously puts you on a fast track to greater effectiveness.
—The Resolutionary

About two years ago I was called in by a rural regional hospital to help the staff with their pervasive attitude of negativity. After interviewing about thirty key managers and providing a day of training about the sources of negative attitudes, we realized that one of the pieces missing from the culture was the mechanism of effective, timely feedback.

Everyone agreed that a negative attitude was pervasive because people were not talking to each other, so rumors were pervasive. Left unchecked, negative statements hung in the air like the elephant in the room. Part of the challenge was to get people beyond their "nice" way of being polite and deferential to each other rather than responding with what they were really thinking. Everyone agreed that it was a great idea to put in place a "culture and environment of feedback." Here's the agreement we generated to get everyone to buy into the feedback game.

Participation Agreement for a Feedback Environment

*1. **Intent and vision:*** Each of us agrees that the negative environment pervading our workplace is in large part the result of unchecked negative and derogatory comments. Our intention is to stop the negativity and turn the organizational culture into an environment of learning and feedback. The specific vision we have is that whenever anyone makes a negative comment, there will be immediate feedback to that person. The feedback would follow principles of effective feedback. The purpose of feedback is learning. Everyone in the hospital agrees to learn how to accept the feedback in a positive way. Our vision for the organization is that through the effective use of feedback, we can change the culture from one of negativity to one of expectation, achievement, learning, and results—a place people look forward to coming to because they are learning.

*2. **Roles:*** We agree that we are responsible for the mood in our work environment. We take the blame for how it has been. We agree to become a group of "open learners" who have given permission to others to provide feedback. We will become stewards of a learning culture. We know we will need teachers who can instruct us in the proper methods of giving and receiving feedback.

*3. **Promises:*** We promise to honor these rules of effective feedback:

- Affect: never when angry or to show superiority
- Time: immediate, when possible and appropriate
- Place: so as not to embarrass anyone
- Language: feedback on behavior, not personality; specific and prescriptive, not evaluative
- Purpose: for learning and improvement

- Receiver: appreciative and thanking
- Perspective: always positive
- Method: like best/next time

4. *Time and value:* We agree that the potential value is enormous for both our professional and personal lives. We agree to keep the feedback culture in place for six months and then evaluate it.

5. *Measurements of satisfaction:* We will measure the following at the end of six months: 65 percent of the unit wants to come to work; absenteeism is decreased by 20 percent; 75 percent of the staff shows up at a voluntary party; laughter and smiling faces are evident in the workplace; the energy in the organization and in the hospital is different.

6. *Concerns and fears:* That people will take the feedback personally and that the hostility, acrimony, and negativity will get worse.

7. *Renegotiation:* We agree to pay close attention to the situation and to change our agreement immediately if things get worse. We agree to put in place a swat team to provide feedback coaching. We agree to dissolve the feedback environment after six months if the swat team makes the assessment that people are not learning.

8. *Consequences:* We agree that if someone makes negative comments without suggesting a better way of doing things they will be assessed a $5 penalty. The penalties will be saved and donated to charity. The intent of the penalty is to create awareness and importance, not to punish. We understand that if our experiment does not work, we will have to continue working in the negative environment we are responsible for creating.

9. Conflict resolution: We agree to the following triage: (1) to self-manage any hostile emotion; (2) to speak directly to the people you are having difficulty with; (3) to call in the swat team to mediate; (4) to defer to a managers advice.

10. Agreement? We agree to participate in creating a feedback environment and to each take responsibility for managing ourselves through the learning.

I checked in periodically on the mood at the hospital to see if levels of productivity had changed. I am pleased to say that anecdotal evidence indicated a huge shift in attitude. People reported a huge increase in energy and many more smiling faces in the corridors. What most people don't recognize is that when learning is taking place, endorphins are secreted by the endocrine system and a euphoria much like a runner's high is generated. To prove this to yourself, think about the last time you found yourself in a very expansive mood because you were learning. Even patients and spouses reported that moods of hospital employees were much improved.

Summary: The purpose of feedback is learning. People need to learn how to accept feedback in a positive way. Through the effective use of feedback, you can shift an organization's culture to an environment of expectation, achievement, learning, and results—a place people look forward to coming because they are learning.

Exercise: Does your organization have a culture of feedback that promotes learning and continual improvement? Is there any plan in place to promote such a culture? Do you think such a plan would be valuable for both the organization and the individuals? Are you willing to accept the challenge of promoting a feedback environment?

CHAPTER 18

DELEGATION AGREEMENTS

● ● ● ● ● ● ●

A manager's accomplishment is directly related to skillful delegation.
—The Resolutionary

Organizations often take their high-performing professional employees (sales people, realtors, programmers, lawyers, draftsmen, designers) and reward them for their achievements by promoting them to manage others. They give them little or no training in management, and even though management competence requires a very different skill set, they expect them to continue being "stars."

Beyond shifting focus from tasks to people, the most important skill a new manager develops is delegation. Simply put, delegation is getting work done through the skills of others. To do that effectively, managers must first break the "I can do it better and faster disease" and learn how to focus on and communicate to the human beings they are managing. This is not easy for high-performing professionals who have been driven by task orientation their entire lives.

The following agreement was put in place by a fast-growing high-tech firm that was promoting people to managerial roles who had little training or experience in managing people. They realized the agreement was necessary because newly promoted managers tended to continue to do the work themselves because that is what they were comfortable with and competent to do. They had little idea of how to delegate or coach people effectively.

This high-tech firm's agreement set up the structure in which new managers had consciousness about *management* competences, as distinguished from technical competences.

Delegating for Effectiveness

1. Intent and vision: To create a group of effective managers who realize they get their work done through others. The vision is to move us managers beyond the tendency to do things ourselves because we can do things better and faster and to realize that delegation of work is a two-way process, not a boss telling someone what to do. The goal is that within six months, managers will stop programming and will be managing others 100 percent of the time.

2. Roles: We are delegators of work. We are also coaches and resources. Our direct reports are our "arms and legs" for getting work done.

3. Promises: We promise to complete a delegation agreement whenever we ask someone to take on a project. This form will include a place for:

1. What is to be done?

2. By when will it be done?

3. How will it be measured?

4. What accomplishments will be observed?

5. Final completion check.

We promise to make ourselves available as resources who teach and guide the people to whom we delegate. We promise to become mentors who resist the temptation to correct things ourselves because we can do it better and faster. We realize that will not help the organization in the long run because it does not transfer our skills to others.

4. *Time and value:* We realize becoming successful, competent delegators is essential for the success of the company and for increasing the value of company stock and thus our stock options. We promise to become successful within three months. We recognize that it is worth our investment of time and energy because of the long-term benefits.

5. *Measurements of satisfaction:* Benchmarks for each manager will be established. Current unit productivity will be measured for each manager. The goal is to increase the current level by 50 percent after three months and 10 percent each month after that, until a 100 percent increase is produced.

6. *Concerns and fears:* Our greatest concern is that we won't be able to let go and make the shift from doing the work ourselves to managing others and that we ourselves will not be given enough training or other learning resources. We are also concerned that we will be losing our leading-edge technological competence as we make this shift.

7. *Renegotiation/dissolution:* The universe we inhabit is moving so fast that flexibility must be our middle name. We agree to evaluate our progress each day and assess who is demonstrating management competence and who might be better suited for technical work.

8. *Consequences:* Loss of value of stock and leading-edge reputation. We will assess $25 for each failure to complete a delegation agreement. We will have a drawing every six months to allocate the funds that accumulate.

9. *Conflict resolution:* A team of managers and technical people will be agreed upon to resolve conflict!

10. *Agreement?* We agree to start playing the delegation game and to see how good we can get at it.

Although the sea change in attitude took about six months to sink in, the performance results were worth the effort. In addition to the agreement, a mentoring and coaching program was established. Managers who had received outstanding feedback from their reports were assigned to new managers. Given the truth that "to teach is to learn twice," both new managers and new coaches reported how valuable the new context was. Not only did everyone learn, but the bottom line was also improved significantly.

Summary: Organizations often take their high-performing professional employees and reward them for their achievements by promoting them to manage others. They give them little or no training in management. Even though management competence requires a very different skill set, they expect them to continue being "stars." The most important skill a new manager must develop is delegation—getting work done through others.

Exercise: Do you delegate at work? Do you think you do it effectively? Why or why not? When you delegate, are you thinking at all about what others will learn? What is the value of delegation—to you, to them, for the enterprise?

CHAPTER 19

BOARD OF DIRECTORS AGREEMENTS

● ● ● ● ● ● ●

Management helps you climb the ladder of success.
Leadership makes certain the ladder is against the right wall.
—Unknown

The mandate of a board is to provide leadership—to make sure the organization is "climbing the right wall." After serving on a few boards, I realized I had never seen any one of them take time to reflect and come up with a comprehensive plan expressing what their work was and how they were to go about it.

As in many other arenas, everyone assumed they knew what they were doing and that everyone else knew what they were doing. It is equally likely that they knew they did not know, but because everyone else was acting as if they knew (which they did not), they were afraid to say anything. I was always somewhat uneasy. I often thought of the classic Abilene Paradox, in which everyone goes along on a horrific automobile ride without protesting, even though everyone thought the trip was a terrible idea—but they just went along anyway.

I suggested it would be a good idea for the board jointly to articulate a road map that succinctly expressed the role it was assuming, where they thought the company was, and the strategic direction they thought was best for the company. As a way of showcasing my work, I volunteered to facilitate a board agreement. Following are the results of that dialogue. At the end of the meeting, one of the members thanked me for the suggestion. He said that the idea was so simple, and yet so profound.

Board of Directors Agreement

1. Intent and vision: It is our intention to provide strategic direction for TEXABRA. Our goal is to reflect on the results and direction of the company and, in consultation between our own and outside directors, articulate a current and timely strategy, as well as a specific vision for the organization. We see ourselves working collaboratively, in committees when needed, to provide management with a strategic direction. Our charge is to assess the health of the organization in the following areas: finance, strategy, marketing, sales, and operations. This board will look at each of these areas whenever we meet as a body.

2. Roles: We will serve as consultants to management. We will listen, advise, monitor, and nudge, all in the name of performance improvement.

3. Promises: We each make the following promises:

- To attend board meetings
- To review management reports before each board meeting
- To be available when necessary between meetings
- To contribute our expertise freely so as to add value to the company
- To hold our board as a learning environment
- To listen to and acknowledge others' contributions
- To do all we can to contribute to the company's performance results

4. Time and value: For each of us, what we receive is more than enough to compensate us for what we expend. Each of us agrees that if we ever feel uncomfortable or unappreciated, we will resign.

5. Measurements of satisfaction: Our success will be measured by the continued improvement of TEXABRA. We will evaluate ourselves on three criteria:

- Pride employees have in products and services
- Presence of healthy, nurturing, and learning relationship
- Financial return on investment—wages for employees and ROI for investors

We will use the traditional measures of for-profit organizations: increased profits, increased volume and market share, brighter prospects for the future, and the opportunity to help create emerging new areas of activity.

6. Concerns and fears: Our primary concern is that, during our watch, the organization will fail to reach its potential.

7. Renegotiation: Our tasks are simple (although not easy), so we do not see much need for renegotiation. As a board, we are already operating in a conceptual, strategic manner. We will change our operational premises if needed.

8. Consequences: The health of the organization, each employee, and the value of the TEXABRA mission are at stake.

9. Conflict resolution: We will continue communicating through any conflict that comes up. We will turn to one another for facilitation if necessary, or to an agreed third party if needed.

10. Agreement? We are a team, all on the same page, serving a mission we believe in.

Having an agreement in place served the board by providing it with a simple reminder of what the function of a board is and what this particular board needed to accomplish. Setting out a strategic agenda allowed members of the board to identify ways in which their individual skills might best serve the organization.

Summary: The function of the board of directors is to assess the health of the organization in areas of finance, strategy, and operations. It is useful for a board jointly to express the role of the board, where they think the company is, and the strategic direction that would be best for the company.

Exercise: Has the board of your organization expressed its mission and function beyond what it is legally required to do by law? If you are a member of a board of directors, engage the board in dialogue to make sure everyone understands their function. If you are part of an organization that has a board of directors, ask them to articulate their mission and their plan for accomplishing it.

CHAPTER 20

STOCKHOLDERS AGREEMENTS

● ● ● ● ● ● ●

This country owes everything to the individual investor. We all share the
indebtedness.
—Unknown

Directly or indirectly, we all share in owning the economy through
our participation in it. Have you ever thought about the responsibility a corporate organization has to its stockholders? There are certain duties required by law. Generally the most important one is the
responsibility to maximize profits. For a growing number of organizations, this responsibility is juxtaposed against some unknown,
amorphous, and unarticulated level of "corporate social responsibility." Under traditional analysis, these values have been considered
adversarial (it's one or the other—one is good, the other is bad).
Greed versus humanistic values. Life versus death. Good versus evil.
I do not think this responsibility is that simple, especially when the
deep concerns of sustainability are added to the mix.

Corporations derive their existence from an enabling law.
There has been a great deal of press about the role of corporations
in an economic system. Some have said that the global corporation, with its impersonal face following the god of immediate profit, is a ticket to the *un*sustainable future we may be creating. They
suggest that corporate charters should be renewable, and that their

extension should be based on some index of social contribution rather than leaving their survival to their continued profitability, which is the current standard.[6]

A few years ago I was asked by a progressive organization, as part of their visioning process, to facilitate a dialogue that would form the basis of an agreement they would extend to their stockholders. I gathered together the board, the senior executives, a number of managers, and a group of representative employees. Every one of them was a stockholder. I asked them to step into the role of corporate operative but to remember that they were also stockholders, citizens of their local community, and citizens of the global community. Here are the results of that meeting.

Agreement with Shareholders

1. Intent and vision: Our intention is to operate a profitable organization while at the same time respecting the values and rights of the community we live in. Our vision is for us to be a respected member of the community who can be counted upon as responsible to the community. We desire to be a new breed of corporate citizen. Profit will *not* be our only motivation, although to remain viable, we must remain profitable.

2. Roles: Everyone who is employed by the corporation agrees that they must continually wear three hats: citizen, stockholder, and corporate operative.

3. Promises: We each promise to act ethically, with integrity and authenticity. We understand that the only way the corporation can act is by and through its employees. We promise to act in no way differently as employees than we would as citizens. We promise to remain conscious of our sense of integrity, no matter what role we are playing. We promise to work hard and make sure our concerns as citizens are voiced. In our role as citizens, we promise to act as representatives for all citizens of the local and global community of which we are a part. We promise to act as stewards of planetary resources and take those into consideration when making decisions about our business operations. We promise to be vigilant in thinking about future generations when we make current decisions.

4. Time and value: We are part of an emerging global experiment. We recognize that holding human and community values as enemies to profitability is not workable. We choose the challenging task of integrating what have been mutually exclusive values. Given the shrinking, interdependent, global village we all share—and the humanitarian stake in terms of human capital and environmental degradation—we agree that the work necessary to make us a responsible corporate citizen is worth the time and effort that will be required.

5. Measurements of satisfaction: We will determine our success under the following matrix: 10 percent increase in profitability annually; local charitable contributions larger than any other giving; no negative PR about our profit-making activities; 90 percent of the workforce will say they are proud of our products and services, as well as the relationships they share at work.

6. Concerns and fears: We are all concerned about polarizing into factions and the tendency to move forward with "profit at any cost" as our driving value.

7. Renegotiation: We sense that this experiment will require that we develop the capacity for ongoing negotiation as we constantly do our best to balance the multiple values we choose to honor.

8. Consequences: We recognize that if our experiment fails, we will be contributing to a polarized world that creates conflict and does not honor humanitarian values when it is not convenient.

9. *Conflict resolution:* We will remain in dialogue with our chairman and use internal and external facilitators as needed.

10. *Agreement?* Yes, although we know we have a daunting task.

Although this document has not yet been made public, it has had an impact on new hires and members of the organization. It makes the statement that "we are aware" of concerns other than profitability and we recognize the international dialogue about sustainability. It recognizes that, although the universe is abundant, like our individual personal ecology, we exist within a context of limited capacity to eliminate the toxicity and byproducts created by our industrial activity. I think this recognition is the leading-edge expression that articulates the views held by many in our culture.[6a]

Summary: Traditionally, stockholders have looked to organizations only for profitability, or return on investment. Progressive and socially responsible investors and stockholders are looking for more than just financial returns; they want the organizations they invest in to be good corporate citizens, defined as time and experience dictate.

Exercise: Select an organization in which you own stock. Do you think they are good corporate citizens? Why or why not? Contact the person in charge of shareholder relations and find out if they have any metrics by which they determine if they are a good citizen. Do you agree with the metrics? Can you suggest others?

CHAPTER 21

STAKEHOLDERS AGREEMENTS

● ● ● ● ● ● ●

After you have exhausted what there is in business, politics, conviviality, and
so on—have found that none of these is fully satisfying or permanent—
What remains? Nature Remains.
—Walt Whitman

When I feel lost or blue, nature is one of the places to which I turn for solace. It does not disappoint. In the past ten years, the concept of *stakeholder* has been getting increasing attention.[7] A stakeholder is different from a *stockholder* or the local community that promotes a standard of social responsibility by serving as a watchdog. The stakeholder is any individual, group, or organization that has a direct interest in the results, activities, or impact of an organization. In ways similar to the responsibility that a corporation owes its stockholders, any venture always has a group of identifiable stakeholders. This is true for a marriage, for a school, for a government entity, for an NGO, and for a business.

Last year I chaired a committee that organized a future search conference for the Law Practice Management section (LPM) of the American Bar Association (ABA). A future search conference is a strategic planning process that seeks to build the future of an organization based on stakeholders' expressed "common ground."[8] Rather than argue then compromise about a direction, the goal is to discover what everyone agrees on and use that as the foundation for the future. The process involves bringing in members of different stakeholder groups who have an interest in the future of the organization. For example, the stakeholder groups for the LPM Future Search Conference included:

- Present leadership of the ABA Law Practice Management section
- Past leadership of the ABA Law Practice Management section
- Present leadership of the ABA
- Consultants to lawyers
- Leaders of law firms
- Lawyers from small-firm environments
- People who are part of the legal services delivery team
- Consumers of legal services (clients)

The following "agreement" between an NGO and its stakeholders acknowledges and demonstrates the value stakeholders bring to organizations. It is more of a pledge by the Balboa Society, but a pledge is a unilateral agreement.

Stakeholder's Agreement

1. Intent and vision: This agreement reflects our intention to honor and acknowledge all stakeholders for the value and contribution they make to the Balboa Society. The vision we have is that they will continue to expand their participation and contribution. They have been especially helpful in volunteering their time in facilitating the design of events that encourage members to explore their inner world. Because of the value they provide to us, our vision is to help them provide the same services to other individuals and professional organizations that our membership belongs to.

2. Roles: We are an organization providing products and services that facilitate individual and group learning. You are facilitators of educational initiatives.

3. Promises: We promise to recognize, understand, and acknowledge the value they bring to the organization. We promise to promote their services when the opportunity arises. We promise, alone and in consultation with them, to look for ways to promote their programs. Promotional activities we promise to do include: announcements, testimonials, opportunities to showcase their activities, inclusion in brochures, and presence on our Web site.

4. Time and value: This agreement will continue in perpetuity. Your continued concern and partnership is clear evidence that we are valued. The Balboa Society believes we receive more than we give.

5. Measurements of satisfaction: We measure our success by the continued input and interest of stakeholders. That is our barometer. We also measure our continuing success by our member interest and activity. We measure success quantitatively, by the number of members who say they are pleased with what we do.

6. Concerns and fears: We have been concerned that our facilitators will stop contributing to programs because we have not acknowledged the value of their contribution.

7. Renegotiation: We will continually negotiate with our facilitators to find ways that enable them to contribute value to our members.

8. Consequences: The stakes are high. Our facilitators can lose a great friend. The Balboa Society might decrease the scope of their influence.

9. Conflict resolution: We will sit in dialogue with our stakeholders to air and resolve any differences.

10. Agreement? The Balboa Society is aligned with our facilitators and ready to move forward from this new recognition of the value that they contribute.

It is important for an organization to articulate an agreement between itself and all of its stakeholder groups, because each has an interest in the other's viability. If there was any doubt, this was made clear to me during the LPM Future Search Conference. The vehicle of agreement is a viable tool for periodically focusing an organization on all those interested and invested in its success. The agreement template can hold the ways in which an organization can articulate the value and importance of its stakeholders for the purpose of engaging a greater level of participation.

Summary: The stakeholder is any individual, group, or organization that has an interest in the results or impact of an organization. In ways similar to the responsibility that a corporation owes to its stockholders, there is always a group of identifiable stakeholders for any venture. An agreement is a vehicle for articulating and encouraging stakeholder importance.

Exercise: Think of an organization or community group of which you are part. Make a list of all the organizations and individuals that are impacted by or have an interest in the viability of your organization. If you have not already done so, invite the identified stakeholder groups to participate.

CHAPTER 22

COMMUNITY AGREEMENTS

● ● ● ● ● ● ●

I am of the opinion that my life belongs to the whole community, and as long
as I live it is my privilege to do for it whatever I can.
—George Bernard Shaw

Organizations, large and small, do not usually think in terms of
George Bernard Shaw's service orientation. Their relationship to
the community they inhabit is not uppermost in their minds. As
Scott Peck says in *The Road Less Traveled,* "Many are called, few
choose."[9] Of course, savvy businesspeople understand the PR
implications of the negative media attention generated when local
concerns are ignored. There are clearly downside PR consequences
when sensitivity and awareness of local concerns is absent. On the
other hand, untapped positive local PR potential is very big.

A corporation is a citizen, a fictitious legal "person" created by
law. It has the right to sue and be sued, it must pay taxes, it must
register and get a license to do business, and it has a legal residence
like a human citizen. From their exercise of conscience, employees
of the Vanguard Group created the following agreement to serve as
the guide and conscience for their organization. When their
process was complete, they reported feeling much better about
going to work and about the context they had created.

Agreement of Good Citizenship

1. Intent and vision: It is our intention to be good citizens of our community—citizens who take more than they give, leaves the place better for having been there, and remain conscious of the impact we place upon physical resources of the community and the natural environment.

2. Roles: We are good citizens looking for ways to contribute, give back to the communities we live in, and be good trustees and stewards.

3. Promises: We request that you promise to be aware of the impact you have on:

- The natural environment and the consumption of natural resources
- The resources you consume, like police, fire, and emergency protection
- Educational resources like schools

We agree to:

- Publicly acknowledge your contributions to the community
- Tell you when we need your help
- Work with you to develop standards with measurable benchmarks to help guide us in this process

4. Time and value: This agreement will stay in force for as long as the corporate entity is alive. We know that we are getting back more than we give.

5. Measurements of satisfaction: We will develop standards to govern our behavior.

6. Concerns and fears: We understand that local citizens may be concerned that we will say the words without taking action.

*7. **Renegotiation:*** As we move forward, we agree to make changes. We realize that we need to know more about what we don't know about our impact so we can monitor all aspects of the local effects of our activities.

*8. **Consequences:*** In many subtle and not-so-subtle ways, civilization as we know it is at stake for future generations when we don't pay attention to the local impacts of our activities. These impacts include use of resources, pollution, cultural changes, and economic implications.

*9. **Conflict resolution:*** When we have conflicts, we will sit in council with local political leaders and citizens.

*10. **Agreement?*** Yes, we can support this charter.

I believe that if more organizations embraced themselves as "responsible citizens" rather than settling for profit-driven machines, we would all feel, and be, less polluted by corporate activities. Rather than focusing on rights, given the shrinking global village, I believe it's time for all of us to focus on responsibilities.

Summary: The great majority of organizations, both large and small, fail to think about their relationship to the community they inhabit, despite the PR implications and the upside potential. If organizations thought of themselves more as responsible citizens than as money machines, we would all feel better about our society. Organizations chartered by law, like individual citizens, could focus on their responsibilities as well as their rights.

Exercise: Do you consider the organizations you are part of to be responsible citizens? What can you do to make them more responsible? Use the agreement model to make a plan with yourself for accomplishing that. Refer to Chapter 31 for guidance.

PART III

• • • • • • •

PROFESSIONAL AND BUSINESS RELATIONSHIPS

• • • • • • •

I started practicing law before legal information was generally and readily available. It was also before legal services were a commodity bought by sophisticated consumers. I remember realizing that my clients did not have much knowledge about the quantity or quality of services I was providing. It also dawned on me that an important part of my job as the "providing professional" was to set expectations about the process and the anticipated results. From my experience, it became clear to me that the initial engagement dialogue, and confirming agreement, were the keys to a successful, satisfying service relationship. As I became a consumer of various kinds of professional services, I noticed how poorly I was being introduced to the process of that particular professional, and how the process was likely to unfold. What follows are agreements for results, which I have prepared for an array of professionals, that have helped to produce for them very satisfied clients, patients, and consumers.

CHAPTER 23

CONSULTANTS

• • • • • • •

The mediocre teacher tells. The good teacher explains.
The superior teacher demonstrates. The great teacher inspires.
—William Ward

Consultants are teachers. Great consultants tell, explain, demonstrate, and inspire. They operate on the premise that it is better to teach someone how to fish than to throw them a fish when they are hungry. Consultants have become an important part of our personal and professional lives. I used to trust the consultants I engaged to manage the consulting relationship by setting appropriate expectations. My assumption was that having done this many times before, they understood the importance of managing the relationship. I have learned through some disappointing experiences that most consultants are no different from the general population. They are not good at establishing a joint vision of the project, setting expectations, and managing the consultative engagement.

Perhaps I'm hypercritical because I am so conscious of the nature of agreement, or perhaps I'm just a demanding client. I know we would all be better served if we had clear agreements that reflect what we currently believe is the road map to the expected results, a clear understanding of the process, and, most important, a clear idea of what may change as we begin the work. As a patient, you always sign a general consent form before a surgical procedure because the surgeon cannot know exactly what will be discovered once the procedure starts. Consulting projects are no different.

Here's an agreement I prepared for resolving management conflicts among six dentists who purchased an office building together.

Letter Agreement

Dear _____:

Thank you for choosing me to help you resolve the conflicts you have been experiencing in the management of your office building. I will do my best to honor that trust. I have done my best to express our conversations in the following letter agreement. Please let me know if you would like to make any changes, corrections, clarifications, or additions.

1. *Intent and vision:* It is our intention to resolve all conflicts that have come up related to the joint ownership and operation of your shared office building. I understand that it is your vision to have in place an agreement that will enable you, smoothly and efficiently, to share the space harmoniously, without conflict or divisiveness, so that you can devote all of your time to practicing your profession.

2. *Roles:* I will be the facilitator responsible for guiding you through the Process of Agreement and Resolution. You will be active participants seeking agreement and resolution.

3. *Promises:*
I promise to:
- Conduct a process called Managing by Agreement
- Speak to each one of you by telephone before the day of the process

- Give each of you the opportunity to share all concerns you have

- Work with you from 9 a.m. until 5 p.m., or later if necessary

- Deliver an agreement that sets forth the resolution of all conflict and an agreement that states your future relationship and the process by which you will run the office building

- Meet with you for a half day sixty days after the initial meeting to monitor your results and address any existing conflict

- Address any conflict and modify your agreement if needed

- Meet, confer, and provide follow-up coaching for you as needed

You promise to:

- Prepare for the meeting by listing your concerns, conflicts, and the behaviors of others you find unacceptable

- Acknowledge the multiple costs to everyone of the current conflicts

- Come to the facilitation and participate fully

- Listen to what others have to say and reflect on your own behavior and how it might be contributing to the difficulty you are having

- Authentically tell your truth about the situation

- Be willing to be educated by what you hear

- Be willing to change your behavior in response to what you hear

- Abide by the new agreement that is reached

- Let go of the conflict, forgive your partners, and step into a new era of relationship

4. *Time and value:* We each promise to put in the time needed to get to resolution and stay resolved. We each understand it is an ongoing and never-ending process. You agree to pay me $10,000 for the services listed above. You acknowledge that this is a fair price for the services provided. You agree to pay $5,000 upon agreement; $2,500 on being presented with your new agreement, and the final $2,500 at the time of our follow-up meeting.

5. *Measurements of satisfaction:* Your partnership is operating without significant conflict. More important, you have the ability to quickly resolve conflict as it surfaces. You develop the ability to quietly smile to yourself when you recall how bad it was.

6. *Concerns and fears:* My concern is that you will not devote the time needed to resolve future conflicts as they arise and that you will not move forward in good faith. You have all expressed the fear that the others are not capable of changing and that you do not know if you are truly capable of letting go of the past.

7. *Renegotiation:* We agree that even though we have been diligent in expressing all the contingencies we can think of, things will likely arise that we did not anticipate. We agree to modify this agreement as needed to meet current realities.

8. *Consequences:* We understand that the failure to reach agreement will result in significant financial loss on the jointly owned building, disruption to individual practices because of having to move, and the sense of loss at having to leave a building everyone likes very much.

9. *Conflict resolution:* If we have any disagreement about our work together, we agree to talk about it. If we cannot resolve it, we agree to select a facilitator to help us get to resolution.

10. *Agreement?* By agreeing to all of what is said in this letter, we have an agreement in place from which to move forward.

I look forward to the opportunity of working with you.

Sincerely,

Stewart Levine

Agreed and Accepted
by_____
    Name   Date

Notice that even though it is a legally binding contract to provide services, it does not look like an imposing formal agreement.
In most situations a simple letter confirming what is understood
and desired, what is promised, and how much will be paid is much
more constructive than a formal-looking document. The content is
the same; the impact is different.

Summary: Consultants have become an important part of our
personal and professional lives. Often they are not very good at setting expectations and managing the consultative engagement. We
would all be better served when engaging a consultant if we had a
clear agreement that reflects a road map to articulated, expected
results and a clear understanding of the process that will get to the
desired results.

Exercise: Think about the last time you used a consultant or had a
consultative relationship. Was the relationship successful? Did you
get what you wanted? Are you currently in a consultative relationship? What is good, and what needs to be improved? Does
the engagement letter inform you of both the process and the
expected results? Why not revise it?

CHAPTER 24

PERSONAL COACHES

● ● ● ● ● ● ●

Losing is safe Winning is scary!
—Unknown

Coach University (www.coachu.com), an online educational organization that trains coaches, has people waiting to get in. It's not surprising, given the culture we live in. Our society is enamored with sports. Metaphors abound: "I really scored," "Time to go on the offensive," "We were beaten up badly," are just a few. If you want to win, you need a great coach. All great players have a coach, so why not ordinary people who are trying to emulate their role models and do their best in a complex world? Personal trainers, motivators, business coaches, and sports and executive coaches are just a few.

Like any other service, the challenge is getting the engagement correct. That means defining the relationship and setting the right expectations. Last year I was asked by a friend to help her design an executive coaching agreement that she could use with her clients. Here is one of the agreements she designed for a client who had the potential for a huge promotion.

Agreement for Coaching Services

*1. **Intent and vision:*** To make Jody Jones the first female, African American CEO of Carlton Savings and Loan Association.

*2. **Roles:*** I will be the coach, and you will be the executive player.

*3. **Promises:***
I promise to:

- Develop a plan with you
- Determine the actions needed to get you from here to the CEO spot
- Review current competencies and develop a learning plan
- Review current relationships; determine who needs to be influenced and how
- Review current projects and responsibilities and determine which ones are high priority, what will constitute success, and how to achieve desired results
- Develop a PR plan
- Work with you twice weekly for the next six months and be available by telephone 24/7 as needed
- Follow up with you to see if you are keeping your promises
- Rehearse and build scenarios for all important conversations
- Coordinate with an image consultant and speech coach as needed
- Push hard, but not too hard
- Get you the CEO slot
- Provide acknowledgement for what you are doing that others do not see
- Develop a plan with intermediate goals

- *Guarantee:* If you do not get the position at Carlton, or an equivalent with another organization, I will return all fees except for expenses I have paid.

You promise to:

- Follow my coaching
- Pay coaching fees on time
- Be a partner with me and recognize that this is not a "Do Me" project
- Be political even if that's not your nature (politics is nothing more than participating in the decision-making process of your organization)
- Dress, speak, interact, and socialize as we agree
- Develop CEO presence—grow "bigger" and more confident
- Be a learner and make those around you part of a learning organization

4. Time and value: You promise to pay me $5,000 on signing this agreement and $2,000 per month for one year.

5. Measurements of satisfaction: Obtaining the CEO position and having a good time doing it; lots of laughter, self-deprecating humor, and learning.

6. Concerns and fears: My concern is that you will become resentful of the things I ask you to do and the conversations I ask you to have. My fear is that you do not have the personal resolve to compete for this position. Your fears are that you will not get the position and that you will jeopardize your career in the process.

7. Renegotiation: We agree to visit the terms of our working agreement monthly to make sure our processes and progress are producing the interim objectives and benchmarks we have developed.

8. Consequences: You will feel the embarrassment of being passed over. I will lose face, reputation, and revenue.

9. Conflict resolution: We will speak directly, and you will consult me as needed.

10. Agreement? We are both excited about this coaching relationship.

Notice the service guarantee. I think it is a great provision to consider. It takes the edge off financial negotiations for intangible services and demonstrates the confidence of the service provider. It also requires a high level of discernment about who you choose to work with.

Summary: Our culture is dominated by sports, and metaphors abound everywhere. If you want to win, you need a great coach. All great players have a coach, so why not ordinary people who are trying to emulate their role models and do their best in a very complex world?

Exercise: Do you use any coaches? Do you have a written agreement with the coach you use? Does it guarantee performance, manage your expectations, and make specific promises about outcomes? How could the agreement and contracting process be improved?

CHAPTER 25

THERAPISTS

● ● ● ● ● ● ●

I have one thing to say, one thing only . . . and I ask you to remember it:
In a universe of ambiguity, this kind of certainty comes only once,
and never again, no matter how many lifetimes you have.
—Robert James Waller, *Bridges of Madison County*

I remember the power with which Clint Eastwood delivered that line in the movie. The quote contrasts the wisdom a therapist friend once shared when I was in a very distressed state. He guaranteed me I would have clarity—AFTER!

I remember reading about the personal therapy experience called *Same Time Next Week*[10] in a memorable book of the same name. The book was written for the public by a therapist who had the same critique for his colleagues as I have for many lawyers. The implication of the title is that people keep coming back next week to talk some more, with no promise or plan for specific results. In other words, people are paying for the professionals to put them through a process without any promise of personal results. Fortunately, consumers have become better educated, and the process of personal therapy is now so commonplace, no stigma is attached. Input from both therapists and patients brings things into the light, and the open discussion has suggested that for many people in therapy a short-term, results-oriented engagement is the best tack.

Having personally experienced a number of therapeutic

modalities, I have come to understand that in situations other than acute pathology, the most important aspect of the process is learning. I believe that framing a relationship with a therapist as educational, not medical, creates a very different context for most people. That said, I do not mean to impugn the long-term work done for people with significant imbalances. Here is an agreement that I designed a number of years ago for a psychologist who worked with morbidly obese women.

Program Participation Agreement

1. *Intent and vision:* Our work together is designed to provide you with very specific tools, both behavioral and emotional. Our goal is to create a new relationship between you and food. Our work is not about examining how bad you feel about being over-weight or theorizing about the psychological causes of which we cannot be certain. Our work is about giving you tools to change your behavior as it relates to food. Our vision is for you to develop a new relationship to food and obesity. Losing weight would be good for health reasons, but it is not our primary goal.

2. *Roles:* I will be the teacher, and you will be the student, although sometimes those roles will be reversed.

3. *Promises:*
I promise:

- To find out all I can about your relationship to food
- To share with you all I have learned about food, eating habits, and eating disorders
- To provide you with a support group
- To provide new ways of thinking about food
- To custom-design for you new behaviors about food
- To meet with you privately on a biweekly basis for six months

- To meet with you in group sessions on weeks I do not see you privately
- To be available by telephone as necessary
- To provide an opportunity for celebrating you, and what you learn

You promise:

- To be on time for all appointments
- To do all your homework assignments
- To complete this six-month educational experience
- To fully and authentically engage with me and all others in the program
- To bring relatives, significant others, and housemates into the program
- To call your "partner" if you are having difficulty with the program
- To pay for the program as promised

4. *Time and value:* This program will be six months long. The cost of the program is $2,000, payable $1,000 at the beginning, $500 after three months, and $500 on the last session. We agree that if you achieve all of what I promise you will be satisfied with what you receive. I am satisfied to deliver myself and my material for $2,000.

5. *Measurements of satisfaction:* We shall measure satisfaction by your movement on two self-esteem indicators, a survey about your relationship to food, your expression of learning, and the observations of someone close to you. If you are not satisfied with the program, you can repeat it for $500 or you can have a full refund.

6. *Concerns and fears:* My concerns are your resignation about your present ability to change your lifelong thinking and eating behaviors. I am also concerned about your potential to fall further into resignation if this method does not work for you. I say this despite a 95 percent satisfaction rate.

7. Renegotiation: We can renegotiate any term, any time. I am open to learning.

8. Consequences: The consequences for me are loss of professional reputation. For you it is depression and obesity-related diseases, both physical and emotional.

9. Conflict resolution: We will listen and speak, soulfully and authentically.

10. Agreement? I am honored you have chosen to participate.

I remember my client reporting to me that the group found the agreement to be useful as a touchstone that kept them on track as they went through the process she had designed. Participants in the program reported that they felt the solemnity of their promises to participate was raised by the vehicle of a signed agreement. It was also a place they could turn to when difficulty arose in their personal experience of the program.

Summary: In the process of therapy, people are often paying for the professional's process, not their own personal results. Fortunately, consumers have become better educated, and the process of personal therapy is now commonplace. Bringing concerns into the light suggests that for many people in therapy, a short -term, results-oriented engagement was the best tack. I have come to understand that an important part of the process is about learning. Framing the "partnership" as educational, not medical, creates a viable, less-threatening learning context.

Exercise: Have you ever been in personal therapy? What was the process like? Do you think promised results would have improved the process? What else would have been useful in managing the process?

CHAPTER 26

PHYSICIANS, DENTISTS, AND HEALTHCARE PRACTITIONERS

● ● ● ● ● ● ●

I found that the quality of care and attention I provided
as a physician was more important than any pill I prescribed.
—Richard Moss, M.D., *The I That Is We*

I have been very fortunate. At age 55, I have had only a few times when I needed to take care of a major healthcare concern. In my interactions with medical professionals I am consistently amazed at the lack of care for the person behind the ailment or injury. For me, the most important information provides me with a context to frame what I will be going through; this gives me a set of expectations that allows me to anticipate what will be happening and become a partner in producing desired outcomes. I am almost always disappointed, despite my best efforts to seek out the information I need.

I do understand the tremendous pressure all healthcare professionals are under within the medical insurance reimbursement system. Reimbursement rates are low, and that requires seeing many patients a day, so time is at a premium. But when I ask specific questions to take care of my expectations and anxiety about the future, healthcare professionals sometimes look at me like I'm from another planet. All I am asking is for them to help alleviate my anxiety by painting a picture of what I can expect. Please help me visualize what's coming so I can partner with you to provide a successful result! What I get instead is a look that seems to say, "Please dumb down. Why are you bothering me, can't you just trust me to do my job?" It seems as if they think I am not attached to my body; I should just make believe it's my car that I'm dropping off for an oil change.

Recently I had arthroscopic kidney-stone surgery. The physical result was great, but the process left a great deal of room for improvement. I can fully understand all the medical malpractice claims, given that I am a professional communicator and that I had to work hard to manage the process. On my initiative, I made a special appointment with the surgeon for the sole purpose of speaking about the process. Without me, it would not have happened, and I can't imagine that.

Although it wasn't life-threatening surgery, it did involve inserting a tube through my side into the kidney to provide access. I was told this would be a simple part of the process, which was understandable, given that it was being done on an outpatient basis. My assumption was that this would be no big deal. WRONG! First of all, I did not know it would be a bifurcated process until I received a call from the hospital to schedule an appointment for the outpatient procedure. I had told my surgeon I wanted the surgery done on Monday. They called to schedule the outpatient procedure for Friday and the surgery for Monday (because they don't work over the weekend). They gave no thought to me spending three days with a wire in my kidney! If the wire was nothing, I might understand that. Given what followed, it is unfathomable.

I quickly tried to provide some input and take some responsibility. I tried to find out if it could all be done at the same time. No. I then insisted on doing procedure one on Monday and the surgery on Tuesday. That was a smart move, given what transpired. I had made arrangements for my sister, a nurse, to be with me for a week during the surgery. She was to arrive the day I had the "real" surgery. My niece was to pick me up after the outpatient procedure and drop me off at home so I could get some work done before being out of commission for a few days. This was my assumption based on what I had been told. Well, it was one of the worst nights of my life, and I have a very high threshold for pain. When my niece dropped me off, the pain was excruciating. She called my sister, who was five hours away, and said, "I don't know if Uncle Stewart is really in great pain or is just a difficult patient."

I could not get ahead of the pain and spent eighteen miserable hours. My sister immediately got into her car and made a hurried trip. All of this could have been avoided with some routine communication that would set clear expectations and take care of the human being going through an invasive process. It is still unbelievable to me that a physician would not think of that. Last year, a friend had the same experience with a foot surgeon. This lack of communication riles me because it's so simple to correct and so obvious that it must be corrected.

The simple way to fix this is to have clear agreements with your healthcare professionals about the procedures and medications they prescribe. Here's an agreement I prepared for a visionary physician in 1989.

New Patient Agreement for Healthcare

1. *Intent and vision:* The intent of our relationship is to provide a context for addressing health and health problems, illness and disease. The vision for results created are cure, relief, awareness, greater health, greater well-being, anxiety reduction, removal of limitation, life enhancement, balance, and peace.

2. *Roles:* You will be the patient who fully participates and is a partner in the healing process. I will be your advocate, trustee, coach/guide, nonjudgmental friend, healer, and confidant.

3. *Promises:*
I promise:

- To listen so I can understand the concerns at issue
- To communicate understandably
- To be respectful
- To be an advocate and trustee for you
- To contribute to your healing and recovery
- To discuss and explore all options openly with you
- To serve as a guide
- To be committed to the best outcome
- To act from determined, dedicated resourcefulness
- To be concerned for your issues and welfare above all else, specifically, above my income or comfort

You promise:

- Honesty
- Cooperation and to follow instructions
- Payment on time
- Respect for the physician's humanity
- Willingness to be healed and full participation
- Personal responsibility

4. Time and value: The relationship created will be ongoing and continue for as long as the specific intended results are produced, or until either of us wants to discontinue the relationship.

- If the physician wishes to discontinue, he agrees to give adequate notice, transfer the case, and be available for emergencies.
- If the patient wishes to discontinue, he will initiate the conversation informing the physician and cancel appointments in a timely manner.

5. Measurements of satisfaction:

- The disease or illness is gone

- There is a maximum diminution of the limitations from the condition and a maximum enhancement of health
- The desired medical, psychological, and social understanding is reached
- All questions are answered
- All fears are addressed and resolved
- Both the physician and patient feel respected and valued
- All uncertainties and unknowns are openly and frankly identified
- The patient is on a path of recovery and healing
- Administrative agreements (fees, appointments, and confidentiality) are honored

6. Concerns and fears:

Of the physician:

- Possible conflicting motivations of the patient: Is a real desire for wellness present?
- Inability to get to the root of the disease
- Patient's inability to understand the disease and its context
- Patient's inadequacy of competence, knowledge, or wisdom
- That either the patient or physician will be passive

Of the patient:

- I will be criticized or devalued
- I will not be heard
- The healing process will be painful and I will experience loss
- I will be forced into awareness of that which I want to deny
- The physician is incompetent
- The physician will lack compassion
- The healing process will require lifestyle changes and will impact family and social relations

7. Renegotiation: The entire relationship is always being renegotiated.

8. Consequences: If we are not successful, the disease process will continue, the patient may die, and the physician will be disappointed or perhaps sued.

9. Conflict resolution: If any breakdowns occur during our relationship, we agree to continue to agree until we reach resolution. If we need a neutral third party, we will seek one to facilitate a new agreement.

10. Agreement? Yes, we have an agreement.

Although long, it is truly artful. Lives are at stake, and therefore it is worth taking the time to create awareness of the true part each person plays in the process. The promises are especially important. But I think that the greatest value it can have is making patients realize they are partners and collaborators in the process of healing themselves.

Summary: When hiring a physician, it is important to ask questions to take care of your expectations and anxiety about the future. You want your physician to alleviate anxiety, painting a picture of what you can expect so you can help visualize a successful result. A personal dialogue leading to a detailed agreement can be very helpful.

Exercise: Make an appointment with your primary care physician for the sole purpose of discussing your expectations of the relationship and how you want to participate. Make yourself available to answer any questions your doctor may have.

CHAPTER 27

REALTORS

· · · · · · ·

Land is a valuable and unique commodity.
They're not making any more of it.
—Unknown

I am often amazed at how little importance people place on selecting a realtor. Next to getting married or choosing a career, the largest decision most people make is the choice to purchase a home. In has, by far, the largest price tag we will ever say yes to. It causes us to incur more debt than we could possibly imagine. Often, the choice of realtor is based on information like "my brother-in-law knows someone who is a realtor."

My advice is to check them out. Do some screening. How long have they been selling real estate? This is critical because the more experience they have, the more effective they will be in reaching an effective and favorable purchase agreement for you. And the agreement can make a big difference. Do they have experience and familiarity with the location you want to buy in? Are they current and familiar with market conditions, financing sources, and creative ways of doing things? Can you trust them? A big thing to look out for is whether they are the listing broker as well as the buyer's broker.

You want a realtor who is fully your advocate. Remember that the commission rate is negotiable. You want to look carefully at the multi-part form they give you. They will not like it, but try incorporating as many of the following terms from an agreement I prepared for a realtor during the superheated market of San Francisco/ Silicon Valley in the late 1990s, when houses were selling for 125 to 150 percent of their listing price. That said—happy house hunting!

Agreement for Real Estate Services

1. *Intent and vision:* It is our intention that within your time parameters, we will find a house for you that meets or exceeds your expectations. We will enjoy the process, and you will be satisfied with the end result. You will return as a client and send other clients to me.

2. *Roles:* I will be the realtor, and you will be the client. We will need others, including a lawyer, financial institution, home inspector, and the municipal code-enforcement officers.

3. *Promises:*
I promise:

- To be your advocate and negotiator
- To be loyal
- To reveal any real or potential conflict of interest
- To listen to what your specific needs are
- To show you only homes that fit your parameters
- To return your calls promptly
- To disclose all financial interests I have in the situation

I ask you to promise:

- To tell me everything you are thinking about in terms of this purchase

- To tell me about all you want in a house and why (it's the only way I can really help)
- To be on time for appointments
- To be immediately responsive to my calls and messages because the market is moving so fast
- To stick with me as this is usually a long-term project

4. *Time and value:* This agreement will be in force until you move into a house with which you are satisfied. If I do my job, you will have the value you are looking for and I will receive a commission.

5. *Measurements of satisfaction:* For me, the best test of a client's satisfaction is referrals. If you send me three referrals within six months from the date you move into your house, I will be satisfied. You have told me that you will be satisfied if we find a house within your budget, if you get into the house on time with no major emotional trauma, and that during the first six months there are no major surprises.

6. *Concerns and fears:* My biggest concern is that I will take you to see many houses and then you will abandon me and purchase a house through another broker. I am also concerned about the current state of the red-hot, super-inflated real estate market and your ability to qualify for a loan, given your financial history. You have told me that your biggest concern is that I will try to get you into a house that is more than you can afford.

7. *Renegotiation:* The entire process is one of ongoing renegotiation as the market and homes available change daily.

8. *Consequences:* If we fail to function as a coordinated team, it will be impossible to stay with the market and find you a house.

9. Conflict resolution: If we have a conflict we can't resolve through talking, we will take advantage of the mediation services of the Alameda County Board of Realtors.

10. Agreement? Yes, we trust each other, and we are ready to move forward!

Summary: Next to getting married or choosing a career, the largest decision most people make is the choice to purchase a home. In has, by far, the largest price tag you will ever say yes to. It causes you to incur more debt than you can imagine. Often the choice of realtor is based on nothing more than the name of a friend of a friend.

Exercise: How did you select a realtor for the last home you purchased? Were you satisfied with the quality of service you received? Are you thinking about purchasing another home? How will you select the realtor this time? What will be different?

CHAPTER 28

BUILDING CONTRACTORS

● ● ● ● ● ● ●

If you refuse everything but the best, you very often get it.
—W. Somerset Maugham

One of the most perilous projects you can get yourself into is home remodeling. I have known people who were out of their house for a year when it was supposed to be three months. Others had to spend twice the amount budgeted. It is even more fraught with the potential for breakdown than building a new home because you are disrupting an ongoing life without something new in place. So, if things go wrong, you end up being suspended in time.

This agreement put the structure on a down-to-the-studs $300,000 renovation of 75 percent of a residence. Fortunately, this was not the primary residence of the owner during the project.

Agreement for Residential Construction

1. Intent and vision: It is our intention to set out our agreement for the rebuilding project at 4598 Lakeview Dr., Spring Valley, New York. We want this remodel to be uniquely easy. Our intent and

vision is for this project to run smoothly and without major difficulty despite the history of remodeling projects.

2. *Roles:* I will be the contractor, and you will be the owner. I will
have similar agreements with all of my subcontractors and suppliers.

3. Promises:

I promise you that I will:

- Provide all options and costs for any decisions that must be
  made
- Be your guide and trusted advisor
- Be your advocate in all dealings with subcontractors,
  suppliers, and permitting officials
- Tell you when I have financial stake in any decision you
  make
- Complete the project on time
- Honor my estimate within a 10 percent variance
- Be responsive to your questions and communications
- Make sure you understand the specific message I am trying to
  deliver

You promise to:

- Pay your invoices on time
- Make decisions within the time frames I suggest
- Make the house available as requested
- Meet with me when I ask
- Be tolerant of the contracting process even when you don't
  want to
- Have patience when necessary

4. *Time and value:* This agreement will remain in force until the
contract is completed. I will do the remodeling for $298,475, plus

or minus 10 percent contingency, using the materials and fixtures specified in Appendix A. I will complete the job within 9 months from the date I start, plus or minus 30 days. You have seen my work and I promise to complete this renovation with the same quality and attention to detail as the one at 4702 Gilmore St. in Spring Valley, New York.

5. *Measurements of satisfaction:* We will measure this project by cost, completion date, amount of conflict, level of laughter, and joy of inhabiting.

6. *Concerns and fears:* I fear that you will not be able to overlook small things despite a very successful project. You fear a major time or cost overrun or a conflict that persists.

7. *Renegotiation:* It will be ongoing and essential to remain in communication at all times.

8. *Consequences:* Bad feelings, loss of reputation, loss of a model of what is possible, loss of friendship, loss of referrals and future projects.

9. *Conflict resolution:* We will continue, locked in a room if need be, to communicate until we resolve the conflicts that arise during this project.

10. *Agreement?* Yes! We have developed a level of trust and believe we will be able to work through difficulties and conflicts that come up in the process.

What's different about building contracts is that you can be sure things will come up that you did not anticipate, or people will just make mistakes. Given the amount of uncertainty, the best edge you have is to make sure you know who you will be "married" to for the duration of the project. As I said earlier, the object of articulating the agreement for results is important, not only for the specifics it surfaces but also, much more so, for the opportunity to get a real sense of who you will be working with and whether you will be able to continue working with and trusting them when (not if) you get into whitewater.

More than in most situations, the tenth element is critical. After all of the agreement details are recorded, the bottomline question is: Do you trust these people in front of you to maintain their integrity, and maintain an even keel when things get difficult? Can you trust them to hang in to resolve things when the going gets tough?

Summary: Remodeling a home can be a perilous project. It is more fraught with the potential for breakdown than building a new home, because you are disrupting an ongoing life without something new in place. If things go wrong, you are suspended in time. You can be sure things will come up that you did not anticipate. Make sure you "know" your contractor.

Exercise: Before remodeling a home, engage in the following exercise in the order indicated: (1) find three people who have been engaged in a remodeling project and ask them about things that did not go well; (2) speak with three people who worked with your proposed contractor and ask them specifically how well they handled any conflict; and (3) have a dialogue and establish an agreement for results.

CHAPTER 29

FINANCIAL PLANNERS

● ● ● ● ● ● ●

To learn that a rich person is not the one who has the most, but who needs
the least. To learn that money can buy everything but happiness.
—An interview with God,
Neale Donald Walsch, *Conversations with God*

In our world today, financial planning has become a critical process. Everyone seems to be concerned with financial freedom, financial security, and what they will need to retire by a certain age with a certain lifestyle. Given the development of sophisticated computer modeling, doing a financial plan is not as complicated as it once was.

The thing to be concerned about with financial planners is their potential conflict of interest. There is no such thing as "free" financial planning if the planner is selling any kind of financial instrument. The best way to do a financial plan is to pay for the services of a licensed professional. Choose one who does not sell insurance, financial instruments, or brokerage services of any kind. Make sure all they are selling is time and advice. Here is a form I designed for a planner who wanted his clients to fill in the blanks.

Financial Planning Service

1. Intent and vision: To make the best possible financial plan.

2. Roles: I will be the listener, planner, financial expert, and trusted advisor. You will be the client.

3. Promises: I promise to listen to your goals, understand your family, honor your values, recommend a plan you can fulfill, and teach you the practical truths about money and finance. You promise to provide truthful financial information, give me the best information you have, honor the commitments you make that are inherent in the plan, trust the plan, and follow my instructions and the instructions inherent in the plan.

In addition, you want me to promise: [write here]

_____

4. Time and value: I am looking for clients for life, clients who will return as their personal or financial situation changes. If I provide a comprehensive plan for $1,500 that satisfies you, I will be satisfied with the value I receive.

5. Measurements of satisfaction: For me the measure is a satisfied client who shared information, listened, asked intelligent questions, was ready to engage with the plan, fulfilled the plan, and achieved the level of financial freedom desired.

Your measurements of satisfaction are: [write here]

_____

6. Concerns and fears: My concerns are that you will not take your financial future seriously, that you will not honor the terms of the plan, that I will be more committed to your financial well-being than you are, or that you will end up in financial difficulty that will contribute to your overall insecurity.

Your concerns and fears are: [write here]

_____

7. *Renegotiation:* We both recognize that we will be uncovering new information as we go through this process and that we will be negotiating as needed.

8. *Consequences:* If you do not honor my plan, or another good plan, you may have difficult financial challenges that could have been avoided.

9. *Conflict resolution:* We shall keep talking until we resolve any differences. I promise never to allow money to harm our relationship. If we cannot reach agreement, we will find a trusted third party to help us.

10. *Agreement?* We have an agreement we can trust!

There is an alternative to financial planning. I have adopted the perspective of being on the continuous journey of discovering what I love to do. As long as I can do that, and be compensated for it, then the idea of retirement never comes up. Why would I retire from something I love! The path has worked for me since 1980, and I'm very pleased with where it's taken me and my expectations for the future.

Summary: There is no such thing as "free" financial planning. The best way to do a financial plan is to pay for the services of a licensed professional. Choose one who does not sell insurance, financial instruments, or brokerage services of any kind. Make sure all they are selling is time and advice. The alternative is to follow your bliss and be well compensated for it.

Exercise: Find a financial planner who meets the criteria mentioned in the summary.

CHAPTER 30

LAWYERS

● ● ● ● ● ● ●

Lawyers spend a great deal of their time shoveling smoke.
—Oliver Wendell Holmes, Jr.

The truth Holmes was pointing to was a lawyer's ability to cloud something simple in the smoke of arcane theory that sounds erudite but no one quite understands. As a "recovering" lawyer, I think I understand most of the nuances of hiring a lawyer. One key to effectively engaging a lawyer is to make sure they can listen and understand the kind of outcome you want. (This is not really unique to hiring a lawyer; the same thing applies to a hair cutter or a gardener.) You want them to listen and follow your instructions. It's your transaction, not the lawyer's. You must choose someone who truly understands that and is willing to be guided by your values, not theirs.

Another key to effective representation is to avoid hourly billing. I believe there is an inherent conflict of interest in hourly billing. It doesn't matter how ethical or righteous the professional is; the conflict is there. This statement is even finding its way into the legal trade magazines as lawyers begin to return to billing based on value of the service provided. Here's a good template to follow when you find the right person.

Legal Services Agreement

1. *Intent and vision:* We will partner as a team to resolve this difficult situation. Our collaboration will effectively take care of your concerns. Your problem will be solved based on your values. Together we hold the vision of you as a happy, satisfied client and me as a fulfilled lawyer.

2. *Roles:* You will be the client and co-collaborator, taking an active role in the process. I will be the wilderness guide, taking you across foreign territory.

3. *Promises:* I promise to listen, understand what you want, be responsive to your needs and communications, confer with you at each choice point, and remember it is mostly your problem, not mostly my case. You promise to be available to strategize and answer questions, tell me the truth, show up for appointments, and pay your fees on time.

4. *Time and value:* We will work together until the matter is resolved. You will pay the sum of $2,500. This will include up to twenty hours of service. If more time needs to be devoted, we will come to a new fee arrangement. We agree that if the matter is resolved for $25,000 or less you will be satisfied with the cost/benefit of the matter and that the value you received was worth it.

5. *Measurements of satisfaction:* Feeling of true partnership, client participation, timeliness of completion, effectiveness of communication, relationship with adversaries, sense of true resolution and completion.

6. *Concerns and fears:* I am concerned you will not collaborate and not make timely financial payments as requested. You are afraid I will not listen and that your problem will become my case.

7. Renegotiation: It will be ongoing as the situation continues to change and develop.

8. Consequences: You will not get the result you want, and I will not get the satisfied client and the testimonial.

9. Conflict resolution: Use the method we learned from Stewart Levine.

10. Agreement? We both believe we can collaborate effectively and be joint problem solvers.

The lawyer-client relationship is no less intimate than a relationship with a therapist. You are trusting another person to be your guide across consequential territory. The more at stake, the more need for real intimacy and trust.

Choose someone who knows how to support other people by being a real partner and teammate. Creativity is not talked about much, but it is essential for getting results in environments that are open to a range of outcomes. Remember to make sure the lawyer is more concerned with serving the situation than serving self.

Look for a confident commonsense innovator who has the empathy to generate openness in others. Look for honesty, integrity, intelligence, good judgment, and for someone who has been down the road before. Life experience about the situation for which you need them is invaluable.

Summary: Choose a lawyer who can listen and understands the outcome you want and who is guided by your values, not theirs. Be careful of the conflict in hourly billing. The relationship is as intimate as with a therapist. The more at stake, the more the need for intimacy and trust. Choose a commonsense, creative, supportive teammate who has specific experience and is more concerned with serving the situation than self.

Exercise: How does your present lawyer stand up against the criteria that were just mentioned? Would you use him or her anyway? Why?

PART IV

• • • • • • •

PERSONAL APPLICATIONS

• • • • • • •

For most people experiencing difficulty with personal relationships, the furthest thing from their mind is the idea of agreements. Therein lies a major cause of the problem! In a professional context, people don't believe their emotions have permission to run rampant. But in the arena of family and personal relationships, emotion is expected to play a bigger part; it is also a greater obstacle to the deep satisfaction we seek in these relationships. For that reason, it is very important to articulate the boundaries in which our emotions can dance. We can do this with agreements when we take the time to express a joint vision, the promises we make to each other, and the standards by which we will evaluate if the relationship is successful and fulfilling our needs.

What often happens is that instead of demonstrating commitment by making clear behavioral agreements as part of designing a highly functional relationship, people get into right/wrong, good/bad, power/submission, and sick/healthy loops. I have found that it's much simpler and saner to make specific behavioral agreements with those you love. What follows in this section are a sampling of personal agreements that demonstrate what's possible. I know how much emotional pain I have prevented by using agreements for results. I have the testimonials to prove it.

A friend told me the story of her mother's second marriage. Without any dialogue on the subject, husband and wife each married for money. And neither had any! That's what can happen when you don't do the work on the front end to put an agreement in place.

CHAPTER 31

AGREEMENTS WITH YOURSELF

• • • • • • •

Why do they always teach us that it's easy and evil to do what we want and that we need discipline to restrain ourselves? It's the hardest thing in the world to do what we want and it takes the greatest kind of courage.
—Ayn Rand

Many people go through life committing partial suicide—destroying their talents, energies, creative qualities. Indeed, to learn how to be good to oneself is often more difficult than to learn how to be good to others.
—Joshua Liebman

I start off this section with two quotes to emphasize the idea that in personal relationships with people we deeply care about, it is not always easy to take care of yourself. Agreements are a way to do that. They require you to be appropriately assertive, taking care of both others and yourself. They require you to have clarity about designing the future of the relationship. They require commitments to action, setting standards, and expressing fears and concerns. Here is an example of using the agreement model to set a goal.

Agreement for Creating My Perfect Job

1. Intent and vision: My intention is create my perfect job, a job that uses all of my skills and competencies. The vision I have is that my creativity will be fully engaged. I will be part of a high-energy team that is working on a project that satisfies my need to innovate and to make a social contribution.

2. Roles: I will be the visionary, change agent, muse, and driver of the project. Others involved will be co-collaborators working in a collegial way. Everyone working on the project will have a unique contribution to make. We will have a finance person, a project manager, a benefactor, and a sales person.

3. Promises: I promise to be vigilant in my search to gather the resources for this project, to seek out people who have similar aspirations, to listen to my inner voice and allow it to guide me to necessary resources, and to stay conscious of the social benefit and maintain that vision.

4. Time and value: This goal embodies my life's work. The return is worth the effort because of the value that will be provided to others. I will be engaged for the rest of my life.

5. Measurements of satisfaction: The energy of engagement, the feedback from others, the level of efficiencies created from operating within a new paradigm, higher levels of productivity, and the emotional cost savings of operating in the old paradigm.

6. Concerns and fears: That I will never develop this project or team.

7. Renegotiation: Ongoing and constant.

8. *Consequences:* I will not be filling my life purpose, those I could be delivering benefit to will not be served, or I will not have the satisfaction of being in and delivering the value of my best work.

9. *Conflict resolution:* I will use the Seven-Step Resolutionary Model.

10. *Agreement?* Yes, I am committed to make this happen and I will stay in dialogue about it!

To most people, the idea of making an agreement with themselves is foreign. It falls in the category of making New Year's resolutions. When teaching, it's the first exercise I ask people to do after explaining the idea of agreements for results. It is an excellent way to get comfortable with the elements of agreement so that when you start working with others you have an understanding of the model, as well as having the experience of using an agreement with yourself. I ask people to think of something they have been putting off for a while; something they have wanted to do or accomplish. The benefit people realize is seeing a way to organize their thinking.

Summary: Making an agreement with yourself is an excellent way of organizing your thinking about something you want to accomplish. The model draws out your vision and the road map to that vision. It provides a path to what you want to accomplish.

Exercise: Think of something you have wanted to accomplish but have been putting off for a while. Make an agreement with yourself about how and when you will accomplish the goal.

CHAPTER 32

AGREEMENTS WITH SPOUSES OR DOMESTIC PARTNERS

● ● ● ● ● ● ●

What have I ever craved more than a woman's arms. To be up half the night,
talking, laughing, making love— have you ever been closer to heaven? The bed
becomes your church; you pass the collection plate back and forth until you've
given too much, then your poverty becomes your gift; your tears, her tears—I
mean, when it's right, who can tell laughing from crying?
—Sy Safransky

Marriage is a 100/100 relationship; unless one is willing
to give everything, one has no chance to succeed in marriage.
Attachment is the expression of lust. Love is the expression of enlightenment.
—Unknown

Relationships with significant others are of profound importance. If something is askew in your primary relationship, it will impact the quality of your work, and all other relationships, including the relationship you have with yourself. Most people don't know where to start, so they never talk about what's bothering them. The agreement I am suggesting is a far cry from what most prenuptial agreements are about: protection, property, and money.

Trying to escape having a serious conversation never works because of the ongoing cost you pay for living in conflict. It is better to have the conversation sooner than later because the conflicts do not disappear. That is why ongoing communication is essential. With the addition of the Domains of Permanent Concern[11], the agreement template provides a solid structure for a primary relationship. Here is an example of an agreement I prepared almost ten years ago for a couple who were about to get married.

Our Marriage Agreement

1. Intent and vision: It is our intention to have a great marriage. This will include fun, romance, travel, financial abundance, friendship, health, partnership, support, and both physical and spiritual love.

2. Roles: Our roles will be mutual. For each other we will be friends, partners, lovers, listeners, and tellers of the truth we each see in situations even if, and sometimes especially if, we know the other will not like hearing it.

3. Promises: We each promise to:
- Stay in the relationship even when it is difficult
- Work things out as partners, realizing that no matter what is going on, we have the same goals in mind
- Stay engaged with the other and continue communicating no matter how difficult
- Accept that if one of us has a problem, then we both have a problem
- Trust the other's good intentions even when we are outraged by what we think they have done
- Be available mentally, physically, emotionally, spiritually
- Make decisions mutually after consulting with each other
- Be warm and affectionate toward each other
- Honor and bring honor to the other

We make the following declarations and promises to each other within the Domains of Permanent Concern:

• *Body.* We acknowledge that our bodies are the sacred temples that house our souls. We agree to respect and honor these temples from the perspective that we each will only get one and that despite the miracles of modern medicine, original equipment is much better than replacement parts, which are not always available. We promise to support each other in healthy eating, physical exercise programs, moderate alcohol consumption, and adequate sleep and rest.

• *Play.* We recognize that the muse of creativity, innovation, and love takes place in the "in-between spaces" of structured activity. Because we function at our highest capacity when we function creatively, we agree to remain mindful of making sure we have enough play time in our lives. For us that will translate into at least two evenings and one afternoon or morning of free play.

• *Sociability.* We understand that although earnestness, diligence, and individual accomplishment are important, real success in life, except for the breakthroughs of a genius working alone, usually comes in the context of society. For that reason we agree to support each other's social engagements and to make it a priority to have ongoing social relationships of both a personal and professional nature. As part of our community involvement and social responsibility, we will be active voices, not passive participants, in the public issues and concerns of the day.

• *Family.* We recognize how essential family is. It is the foundation of a strong social culture. We know that we are defined not only by the roles we choose but, more important, also how we are recognized and defined by others. Despite the risk of bringing children into an unsettled world, we want to build our own family with at least two children as the center of our lives. We also want to nurture our ties to both of our extended families.

• *Work.* We each understand the value and importance of work. Work is a joyful contribution. It also pays the bills. We agree to support each other in making sure that neither of us has to be engaged in work purely for a paycheck, although we both recognize that it is necessary for us to support our family.

• *Education.* Ours will be a house of lifelong learning. We recognize that to be human is to learn. We promise to support each other's continuing education, be it academic or experiential.

• *Career.* We value a planned career. A career is a lifelong pursuit of work in an integrated fashion. By *career* we mean developing a body of work that leaves behind a legacy of substance that is a contribution to an existing body of knowledge or a professional discipline. We agree to support each other's career choices even when we don't fully understand them despite ongoing dialogue.

• *Money.* We say that money is a means to an end, not an end to itself. Money is a medium that facilitates exchange transactions. Money helps to provide freedom from economic worry, creature comforts, freedom of movement, and financial security. Given our views on education, career, and work, it is clear that for us money is a means to other things.

• *Membership.* We will demonstrate our support of certain values and causes by the organizations we join, as a couple and as individuals. Because of the impact it has on the other, we will consult with each other before taking on leadership roles.

• *Situation.* We define *situation* as the assessment we make individually and collectively of our relative situation at the moment. We will look at all of the domains of concern periodically and make an assessment of our situation. We will do this for the purpose of deciding how we are doing in general and what action needs to be taken to keep us on a path toward our vision. The result of evaluating our situation will be an action plan.

4. *Time and value:* We agree that if we are achieving our vision, whatever we devote to our marriage will be worth it. For us it is a lifetime commitment.

5. Measurements of satisfaction: Achieving, or on the way to achieving, 80 percent of our vision. We say 80 percent because we have aimed high. We promise to develop specific measurable benchmarks for each element of the vision.

6. Concerns and fears: That we will grow tired of each other, that one or both of us will change dramatically, that our vision is not achievable, that we will fail to keep our agreement current, that we will loose touch with each other, that either of us will become fascinated with someone else.

7. Renegotiation: We agree constantly to renegotiate all aspects of our relationship.

8. Consequences: If we fail, we will be unhappy; our ideals will be compromised; we will be disillusioned to the point of depression, withdrawal, and inaction; our identities will be compromised; we will lose our best friend and confidant.

9. Conflict resolution: We recognize that the best antidote to conflict is changing the game. We will keep talking, we will never go to sleep angry, and we will work with the models in *Getting to Resolution.*

10. Agreement? We are thrilled to be looking to the future, having discussed all of the above.

The agreement is inspirational, aspirational, and practical. It is useful both as a model of what is possible and as a talisman to consult when you get off track. I have heard from this couple periodically over the last ten years. They tell me that the "agreement stuff" really works. When they're challenged as a couple, they head for the mountains and revise their agreement.

Summary: Relationships with significant others are of profound importance. If something is askew in your primary relationship, it will impact the quality of your work and all of your other relationships. Most people don't think about having agreements for personal, intimate matters, so they never create clear understandings. With the addition of the Domains of Permanent Concern, the agreement template provides a solid structure for a primary relationship.

Exercise: Use the agreement template to craft an agreement for your primary relationship. Even though it is frightening to open the conversation, do it anyway.

CHAPTER 33

AGREEMENT ENDING A MARRIAGE

• • • • • • •

In love's service only the wounded can serve.
—Thornton Wilder

I get a great deal of satisfaction from the work I do. I always feel especially fortunate and gratified when I work with a couple to help them put in place an agreement that will end the legal aspects of their marriage. The relationship itself is in the hands of other forces, although many people, unfortunately, don't understand that. Here is an example of an agreement I recently drafted after working with a couple for one day. This is a representative sample of many I have prepared in the past twenty years. Clients often report that even though they are not together, the process created emotional completion for them, leaving them with fond memories of a person they chose to love even though that love has changed. This takes on monumental importance when children are involved.

Memorandum of Understandings (MOU)

On May 14, 2001, Arnold and Joanne Hill met with Stewart Levine at 1275 Hollyhock Lane, Bellmawr, New Jersey, to resolve their marriage, separation, and divorce. It was understood that all discussions took place in the context of mediation with any and all legal protections attaching.

The resolution is based on the following agreed facts:

1. Joanne was born on July 27, 1965, and is currently residing at 1275 Hollyhock Lane, Bellmawr, New Jersey. Joanne is employed in the real estate business and earns $51,000 per year. Her workplace provides health insurance benefits for herself and daughter Beth.

2. Arnold was born on March 29, 1963, and is currently residing at 28 Dawn Court, Cherry Hill, New Jersey. Arnold is employed as a stockbroker and currently earns $185,000 per year.

3. Joanne and Arnold were married on May 15, 1986. They have one daughter, Beth, born July, 24, 1992.

4. Joanne and Arnold have been living separate and apart since February 2000.

5. Joanne and Arnold have made full and complete disclosure to each other of all assets and income.

Joanne and Arnold agree as follows:

1. They will be changing their relationship from husband and wife to "old friends." They choose to honor their many years together by remaining friends and jointly taking on the responsibility of raising Beth.

2. Together they agree as follows:

(a) They shall have joint legal and physical custody of Beth, sharing all parenting decisions. Each shall have physical custody of Beth for approximately 182 days per year. They shall each have Beth on alternate weekends, Friday to Sunday. They shall agree on specific days during the week as is convenient for them and Beth, with the understanding that Joanne will be Beth's day care on Monday. Joanne shall have Beth for Easter and Christmas Eve. Arnold shall have Beth on Christmas Day. They shall both be with Beth on Christmas morning and Beth's birthday. They shall alternate Thanksgiving, with Joanne going first. They shall alternate Memorial Day, July 4, and Labor Day, taking into account regular weekend visits. They shall fully cooperate with each other about scheduling, and planning vacations.

(b) Arnold agrees to pay Joanne $1,000 per month alimony for a minimum period of twelve years, or until she remarries, or establishes a domestic partnership. If Joanne has not remarried or established a domestic partnership at the end of twelve years, they agree to discuss the matter at that time. This provision reflects their inability to finalize an ending time for alimony.

(c) Arnold agrees to pay Joanne $220 per week, or $952 per month, for child support.

(d) Joanne is responsible for paying for child care.

(e) Arnold shall be entitled to declare Beth as a dependent. This is purely a financial decision and in no way reflects on custody or parenting decisions.

(f) Joanne and Arnold will file joint tax returns for 2001 and 2002.

(g) The following joint assets shall be equitably distributed in the following manner:

- The marital home, worth approximately $375,000, located at 1275 Hollyhock Lane, Bellmawr, New Jersey, shall be immediately sold, the mortgage to First Savings of $188,000 shall be paid along with all other expenses of sale, and the proceeds shall be divided equally between Joanne and Arnold.

- Arnold's Fidelity 401(k) plan, worth $72,000 as of April 30, 2001, shall remain his sole property.

- The American Century Ultra Fund, worth approximately $5,359, shall be used for joint expenses related to the separation.

- Arnold's childhood Pfizer ($13,281) and Disney ($2,800) stock shall remain his sole property.

- The 1999 Maxima automobile shall be Arnold's sole property. He shall pay the First Savings home equity loan balance of approximately $4300 that was used to finance the automobile.

- The 2001 Mercedes automobile shall be Joanne's sole property. She shall pay the loan balance of approximately $14,000 to Capital Credit.

- Personal property shall be divided as Joanne and Arnold agree, with the following specifically going to: *Joanne:* piano, exercise equipment, ritz poster, Beth's furniture, stereo, office furniture, pew, pinball machine, sofa, Fiestaware, cooking equipment *Arnold:* "Saks" stuff, Kitty on Boat, dresser, guest room, dining room

- Gardening equipment will be divided equally.

(h) At such time as they have the legal right, either may pursue a no-fault divorce.

(i) If Beth's college expenses are not otherwise provided for, Joanne and Arnold agree to share the expenses of an undergraduate education in proportion to their respective incomes at the time Beth begins college.

3. Joanne and Arnold believe that the agreement they have reached is fair, and they each move forward with confidence that they have treated each other, and the memory of their marriage, honorably.

4. If circumstances change, Joanne and Arnold agree to make

requests of each other as may be appropriate. They do not wish to deal with those contingencies now.

5. In the event a conflict or disagreement arises about any part of this agreement, or any aspect of the marriage, divorce, or parenting of Beth, Joanne and Arnold agree to confer with each other before seeking the help or counsel of any third party. If they cannot reach agreement, they agree to engage a mediator to resolve their differences.

Agreed and Accepted:

_____   _____
Joanne Hill   Date   Arnold Hill   Date

I wish that more people would stop using the divorce process to play out their unresolved emotional hostilities. Reaching an agreement can be a simple thing, if only people will let go, forgive, and realize that usually things happen for reasons that are revealed in the future—but we can only see them if we have the courage to stop holding on to the past so tightly. This agreement reflects a couple who had the ability to do that. It looks a bit different from others in this book because it will become part of their divorce proceedings, but when you look at it closely, it contains all of the essential elements.

Summary: A great deal of pain and suffering could be avoided if more people stopped using the divorce process to play out their own personal emotional issues. Resolving financial and property issues related to a divorce is best seen as "business" negotiations that define new financial relationships. Let go, forgive, and make a new agreement. A new agreement is all the judge will give you.

Exercise: Suggest to someone you know who is about to go through a divorce that there is a better way than a battle. Explain to them the value of reaching a voluntary agreement.

CHAPTER 34

A NUCLEAR FAMILY AGREEMENT

• • • • • • •

Love is saying yes to belonging!

—David Steindl-Rast

Most people cringe at the thought of having a family agreement. They can't imagine children participating in designing a vision of the family they want to be part of. Over the years, I have found that kids are much smarter and wiser than we give them credit for. This is especially true today, given the content of all the media to which kids are exposed. A few years ago, I overheard my friend's kids complaining to their parents that their family life was not as much fun or as rich as some of their friends. I volunteered to facilitate the following family agreement.

Our Family Agreement

1. Intent and vision: Our intention is to design a context for our family life. We all want the time between now and the end of college to be an engaging, fun, open learning experience that provides the foundation for lifelong family and friendship. Some of the specific things in our vision are family vacations; family learning subjects; family discussions that allow the adults to be people, not just parents; space for our friends to come over and hang out; no taboo subjects; feelings of warmth, nurturing, and honest discussion; a place we can be totally ourselves; a place that is safe.

2. *Roles:* Jean and George will be parents and people. Jean will take charge in the house, not because she is the mom but because she has the skills; George will take charge outside the home because he has that kind of take-charge competence. Bret and Bradley will be kids, but they will also get recognition as young people who have a voice, with opinions that contribute to the family dialogue.

3. *Promises:*
We all promise to:
- Listen to each other
- Be educated by what others say
- Make joint decisions as a family
- Hold family time as sacred
- Schedule real play time with each other
- Hold each other as important
- Take care of each other's needs
- Recognize the ways in which we are different
- Acknowledge the ways in which we have different needs
- Divide and share chores around the house
- Remember that we are building a foundation for the future

4. *Time and value:* If we realize the vision of what we want to be as a family, we believe our effort and the time we devote to family will be worth it. We will stay in this agreement for the rest of our lives.

5. *Measurements of satisfaction:* We will each conclude that, objectively, we are doing the things that a family does and that, subjectively, we all feel we have a place to come home to that is comfortable, supportive, nurturing, and allows us to be who we are. We agree that every six months we will make a list of what we think a family does.

6. *Concerns and fears:* Each of us is concerned that in the fast-paced world in which we live we will not make the time to be with each other as a family because of all of our varied outside interests. Jean and George are afraid that Bret and Brad will rebel from the expressed and implied responsibilities of this family agreement.

7. *Renegotiation:* We all understand that to be successful in this experiment, we will have to be flexible. We all agree to keep talking about changes we must make all the time.

8. *Consequences:* We realize that the consequences of not being successful will be that we will not have a foundation of real family as we get older. We understand that to be close, we have to get close.

9. *Conflict resolution:* We will continue to talk until we are no longer in conflict, no matter how long it takes. We will use the Resolutionary Model.

10. *Agreement?* We are excited by the idea that we can have an impact on the experience we have as a family.

It was a wonderful experience for everyone. All participants learned a great deal, especially Jean and George, the adults. Bret (15) and Bradley (13) demonstrated how much they knew and understood. One of the things everyone learned was how much young people crave context and boundaries. They have all reported how the process opened up new paths of communication and gave them the gift of not being afraid to engage in dialogue.

Summary: Just as you can put in place an agreement for a primary relationship, you can do the same for a nuclear family. Kids are much smarter and wiser than we give them credit for. Young people crave context and boundaries, and an agreement provides that for them.

Exercise: Ask your kids if they want to craft a family agreement. If they do, craft one.

CHAPTER 35

AGREEMENT WITH EXTENDED FAMILIES

● ● ● ● ● ● ●

Happy is said to be the family which can eat onions together. They are, for
the time being, separate from the world, and have a harmony of aspiration.
—Charles Dudley Warner, *My Summer in a Garden*

I grew up in a large ethnic family. My father was part of the "family business" that was started by my grandfather. Each of my parents came from four-sibling families. Although my aunts and
uncles were not prodigious, I was part of a group of eleven first
cousins who were all living within a ten-mile radius. Until the end
of grammar school, I spent entire summers living in the same
house as six of my cousins. I understand by direct experience what
it's like to live in an environment that does not honor boundaries
and privacy. It's not that people were invasive, they were just an
omnipresent part of the fabric of life.

A few years ago I was called by a third-generation farming
family. The family consisted of four siblings and their spouses, who
all worked on the farm. Every nuclear family had a house on the
property and worked the family farm under the guidance of the
patriarch while the matriarch ran the farm office. Some specific
family conflicts arose related to the operation of the farm. After
spending a morning listening to them, I suspected they were all
suffering from claustrophobic togetherness.

My intuition and experience told me that their conflicts would move toward resolution if they put in place a specific agreement setting up some rules about how they would communicate with each other. This reflected my highest ideal—that if you have conflict, the best resolution is a new agreement for the future. I have found that is the best way both to solve a problem and to get around useless processing of the conflict (determine right/wrong, win/lose, and fault/blame). This only works if everyone understands that it requires giving up the need to be right and is willing to forgive and let go of old conflicts. The strategy was a good one, measured by its effectiveness. Here's the agreement we designed.

Smithfield Family Agreement

1. *Intent and vision:* It is our intention to reduce the tension and friction between members of this family. Our vision for the future is to have an effective family farm operation that (a) we can be proud of in terms of our reputation in the community, (b) is satisfying in terms of the relationships we have with the people we work with, and (c) is financially rewarding in terms of both current income and asset appreciation.

2. *Roles:* We all recognize the complexity of the roles, relationships, and stereotypes we are dealing with. To each other, we are siblings, spouses, parents, in-laws, bosses, direct reports, and coworkers. We see that the opportunity exists for all kinds of tension and turmoil if we do not stay mindful of the complexity in which we live.

3. *Promises:*
We each promise to do the following:

- To enroll, attend, and discuss the community college communications workshop at our end of workday

Wednesday meeting (after nonfamily employees have gone home)

- To become learners and observers of each other and to recognize our opportunity for learning, personal growth, and financial reward

- To stay mindful that we must let go of our childhood perceptions and prejudices about each other

- To realize that the only way we will be able to survive and keep the farm is if we treat each other as adults and treat the farm as a business, requiring everyone to take on the role of a dedicated adult employee acting as if this were *not* a family business

- To cancel our shared annual two-week family vacation for the foreseeable future because what each needs right now is some respite from the intensity of our multilayered relationships

- To seek recreation and friendships outside of the family

- To treat each other with dignity and respect

- To listen actively to what others are saying

- To think about what is fair and best for everyone in a situation

- To develop a spirit of teamship

- To honor and acknowledge what our parents have built for us

- To recognize that given current economic conditions within the farming community, if we do not pull together we will lose what we have

4. Time and value: We hope to stay within this agreement for the rest of our lives. We recognize this may not be possible. We all agree to live within the promises we make for one year and then we will assess whether we should continue. We all believe that given the upside potential, it is worth the effort.

5. Measurements of satisfaction:

- Everyone is speaking to each other.
- No one is slamming doors.
- We experience reduced anxiety and tension.
- Absenteeism improves by 50 percent within six months.
- Profits improve by 50 percent within one year.
- We begin voluntarily to socialize with each other.
- We achieve renewed appreciation for each other's talents, skills, abilities, unique gifts, and contributions to the family enterprise.

6. Concerns and fears: That we will not be able to get beyond our emotions and step fully into today, and adulthood, to realize what is possible; that all of us will not be able to learn fast enough; that we have done too much damage; that it might be smarter to divide or sell the farm; that all of us are not committed to making this work.

7. Renegotiation/dissolution: We all recognize that operating within this new context is an experiment that will likely need renegotiation and coaching as we discover how each of us individually reacts to it and as we do our best to honor it. We understand that we are trying to create new operating relationships and that we must be fluid if they are to succeed.

8. Consequences: We have the potential to lose our way of life, our family, and our livelihood.

9. Conflict resolution: (a) We will talk with each other; (b) we will talk with our farm manager and good friend, Ralph; (c) we will call Stewart Levine.

10. Agreement? Yes, we have little choice, given the risk of loss.

I was contacted by the oldest son three years after we worked together. He wanted me to help the family come to agreement about structuring a way to divide the proceeds from the farm's purchase by a large, "corporate" farmer. I am pleased to report that it was not a difficult facilitation. The ground work we did in opening up communication paths enabled a real dialogue to take place about the future and everyone's needs. All were satisfied with the end result.

Summary: Conflicts can disappear if you put in place a specific agreement for setting up some rules about how a large extended family will work together and communicate with each other. When you have conflict, the best resolution is a new agreement for the future. That is the way to both solve a problem and avoid the need to process the conflict. But it only works if everyone involved is willing to stop being right, forgive, and let go of old conflicts.

Exercise: Do you have an extended family that you love but often find intrusive? Construct a family communication agreement following the agreement in this chapter.

CHAPTER 36

AGREEMENT WITH PARENTS

• • • • • • •

Are you placing your wants before the needs of others?
—Viking Runes

One of the most difficult transitions for a family to make is accepting the reversing roles as parents get older. It is one thing to have a living will to deal with healthcare concerns; it's another to speak openly about the transition by which adult children take on a parental role for their own parents. The articulation and dialogue surrounding the design of a structure to make this transition seamless are very delicate. I have done a few of these, and they require an exquisite sensitivity. There is obviously a built-in level of resistance by everyone: parents want to remain in control, and adult children still want to be kids. Here's an agreement you can consider.

Family Transition Agreement

1. *Intent and vision:* Our intent and vision is to preserve the relationship we have while providing for an orderly transition by speaking honestly about the future. Specifically, the vision is to have parents feeling well taken care of and children feeling responsible. We all want to speak openly about difficult and sometimes painful matters.

*2. **Roles:*** As part of the family life cycle, parents will become as children in the sense of being taken care of, and children shall assume the role of caretakers for their aging parents. Other professionals will assume such roles as are necessary for a smooth transition.

3. Promises:

We all promise to:

- Listen carefully and be educated by what we hear
- Respect what we are trying to accomplish
- Trust each other
- Ascribe the highest of motives to everyone
- Go slowly in the assumption of our new roles, absent some extraordinary or catastrophic event
- Be vigilant in observing parents' continuing ability to live independently, drive an automobile, take care of each other
- Treat protests with dignity and discernment
- Explain and avoid edicts

*4. **Time and value:*** We have no doubt that the value of a smooth transition will be worth the time of structuring this agreement and tending the garden it creates.

*5. **Measurements of satisfaction:*** Transition without acrimony, high level of trust and respect, and a great deal of love and nurturance.

*6. **Concerns and fears:*** That there will be resistance, and a resistance to the resistance, making the process highly emotional.

*7. **Renegotiation:*** It will be a continuing part of the process.

8. *Consequences:* We will not have the transition that is possible. A rift will take place in the family.

9. *Conflict resolution:* We will bring in a third party if emotions run too high in our dialogue.

10. *Agreement?* We have reached an understanding.

It takes a great deal of maturity and reflection to engage in the dialogue, prepare the agreement, and honor its terms. Much more important than the agreement is the dialogue. Getting out in the open what often lurks just beneath the surface is very healthy.

Summary: One of the most difficult transitions for a family to make is accepting the reversing roles as parents get older. It is one thing to have a living will to deal with healthcare concerns; it's another to speak openly about the transition by which adult children take on a parental role. An agreement is a useful tool for design of a structure to make this transition as seamless as possible.

Exercise: If you have aging parents, see if they are open to a dialogue about their readiness and willingness to be cared for in a different way. See if they are ready to give up some control and autonomy.

CHAPTER 37

AGREEMENT BETWEEN PARENTS

● ● ● ● ● ● ●

Most people receive very little training on how to live effectively and harmoniously with themselves and others. This I believe is an unfortunate outcome of our parenting beliefs and methods [that] emphasize academic and vocational skills and place little or no emphasis or value on providing a person with the essential skills to live a life of personal fulfillment, contribution and self actualization. . . . Without proper training on how to make wise choices in one's life, the chances are very slim anyone will make them.
—Sidney Madwed

A great deal of uncertainty and insecurity for kids can be caused when parents are constantly arguing, disagreeing in response to kids requests, and allowing a child to play one parent against the other. A few years ago, I was involved with just such a family dynamic. The teenage son, Roy, had acted out self-destructively. The adults in the household were highly intelligent, super-competitive, type A professionals. Unfortunately, in front of their children, they were always competing with each other, and each of them always had to be right.

I was asked to intervene after Roy had been arrested and placed in a treatment facility with a detox program. Here's the agreement we came up with.

Cooperative Positive Parenting

As a result of the current family crisis with their son, Roy, Harriet Green and Mark Green desire to be more effective parents in the future. They met on November 18 and reached the following agreements and understandings.

1. *Intention and vision:* We want to create an environment of Creative Positive Parenting. The specific vision we have of Creative Positive Parenting includes the following:

- Children are our first priority.
- Respective work and careers are not the highest priority in our triage situation.
- We will allow Roy to ask all the questions he wants and we will respond as best and as openly as we can.
- We will listen to each other's concerns.
- We are each bankrupt when it comes to our respective emotional bank accounts and we agree to be conscious of making daily deposits in our accounts with each other.
- We will manage our emotions when we are triggered by each other.
- We will provide a foundation of unconditional love for Roy.
- We will insulate Roy from any of our historic conflict.
- We have happy, joyful children.
- We set the mood and tone in which our family flourishes.
- We are intimately involved with life decisions made by Jane and Roy.
- We will become excellent listeners.

2. *Promises/requests:* We make the following promises to, and requests of each other, that:

- The focus remain on Roy in the immediate future, including our trip to see him in Denver

- We consult with each other on all decisions about Roy and Jane

- We communicate with Roy that we are seeking help with our conflicts and communication patterns, just as he is seeking help

- We will not disagree with each other in front of Roy

- We will not roll our eyes when we think the other said something dumb

- We will check in with each other about whether Jane and Roy are playing one of us off against the other

- We will not gloat when Roy criticizes the other

- We will each do something nice and thoughtful for the other every day

- We will use "I" messages when commenting on the other's behavior

3. *Value:* We believe that making our vision a reality and honoring our respective promises are worth it in terms of what we will get back, including:

- Making the best we can of a very difficult situation

- Relaxing ongoing tension

- Devoting energy and time to the decisions about our marriage

- The possibility of having an ideal family life

- Knowing we did our best from this point forward

- Taking care of Roy

- Helping Jane make some important decisions about her life

4. *Concerns/fears:* We have the following concerns and fears about our ability to honor this agreement, achieve what we want, and keep our promises:

- We have not been able to do this in the past.
- We will revert to hiding from our personal accountability.
- Jane and Roy will suffer the negative consequences of our splitting up.
- Mark will quit his job to devote himself to family concerns.

5. *Measurements of satisfaction:* We will evaluate our success under this agreement by the following standards:

- Harriet believes Mark is emotionally engaged and sees the big picture of things.
- Mark feels comfortable talking with Harriet and is not afraid she will scream at him or be overly critical.
- It is enjoyable to be with Jane and Roy.
- Jane and Roy enjoy bringing friends over because the environment is hospitable.
- Harriet and Mark can have a real dialogue at the end of the weekend they pick up Roy.
- There is a reduced level of hostility and tension.

6. *Consequences:* If we are not successful at living up to this agreement, we realize we will pay the following consequences:

- We will split up and carry the same communication problems into new relationships.
- Roy may feel that he triggered the separation.
- We will experience continued unpleasantness.
- It will have a negative impact on Roy's recovery and Jane's life.
- The waste of time of our dysfunction.
- Roy will never be able to come home.

7. *Renegotiation:* We each understand that circumstances will arise that we did not think about before. We recognize the physical and emotional costs of unending conflict.

8. *Agreement:* We believe we have an agreement that is expressed in these pages. We agree to follow the terms of this, our agreement.

Agreed: Agreed:

/s/_____   /s/_____

Harriet Green   Date   Mark Green   Date

I worked with Harriet and Mark in a way that would enable them to present a unified front around caring for their son, leaving their baggage as a couple at home. It was a challenging intervention, but it worked very well. All have reported that, although things are not always easy, they now at least have a context in which to communicate.

Summary: A great deal of uncertainty and insecurity for kids can be caused when parents are constantly arguing, disagreeing in response to kids requests, and allowing a child to play one parent against the other. Once parents realize they are negatively impacting their kids, it can be very useful for them to agree on how they will conduct themselves in front of their kids.

Exercise: Do you argue with your spouse a great deal in front of your kids? How do they react? What can you see on their faces? Have you ever spoken to them about it? If you and your spouse agree that the behavior is destructive, try reaching agreement about it.

PART V

• • • • • • •

CREATING A CULTURE OF AGREEMENT AND RESOLUTION

• • • • • • •

It's nice to understand something about agreement. But that's only the beginning, the first step—and the easiest step! The ideas are simple, but the work is not easy. The challenge is in the implementation, taking the time to weave agreements all through the fabric of your life, in your home, in your workplace, and with those you serve and those who serve you. It requires a certain strength and intentionality, but the rewards are worth the effort. This section begins with the benefits of living in a Culture of Agreement, provides a context showing how agreement and resolution are part of the same cycle, and gives you some critical tips for moving forward, both affirmatively and as coaching responses to the likely resistance you will encounter.

As you move through this section, please first think about making an agreement with yourself to create the Culture of Agreement around you, then think about who else you need as partners to fill your world with all the value that's waiting.

CHAPTER 38

THE BENEFITS OF A CULTURE OF AGREEMENT

• • • • • • •

Whatever failures I have known, whatever errors I have committed,
whatever follies I have witnessed in private and public life,
have been the consequences of action without thought.
—Bernard Baruch

Putting agreements in place in all your endeavors is the antithesis of "action without thought." Having agreements is a *response*, rather than a reaction, to a situation. Having agreements, and honoring their terms, is a way to avoid the consequences of reactive behavior that has no context. The benefit of a Culture of Agreement is dual: one is the incremental value of desired results, the other is avoidance of the negative costs of conflict. Let's look at the negative side first.

The Cost of Conflict

We need to look at the unseen, unarticulated, and significant costs of conflict. When relationships are not consciously created, and conflict is not prevented with agreements for results, the potential for litigation greatly increases. Last year more than 22 million cases were filed in U.S. courts, at a cost of almost $400 billion.[12]

Executives spend more than 20 percent of their time in litigation and conflict resolution–related activities. Imagine the cost in lost productivity and opportunity! It is commonplace for legal fees to exceed the value of the amount at stake. Years ago, if a situation had more than $100,000 at stake, litigation was a viable alternative. Today the benchmark is $1 million and growing quickly. Following an old paradigm is very costly!

The cost of conflict represents a resource drain of huge proportion and a source of great unhappiness and discomfort. Because they are often invisible, it's important to identify and understand all of the costs of conflict and to examine some tangible examples. My hope is that recognizing the extensive costs of conflict will motivate conflict prevention through the use of agreements for results.

The cost of conflict is composed of the following:

1. *Direct cost:* Fees of lawyers and other professionals

2. *Productivity cost:* Value of lost time and the opportunity cost of what the people involved would otherwise be producing

3. *Continuity cost:* Loss of ongoing relationships, including the "community" they embody

4. *Emotional cost:* The pain of focusing on and being held hostage by emotions that results in the inability to focus completely on what is happening in the present moment

Direct Costs

Because of an inability to face conflicts, many people spend money they can't afford on lawyers hired to do their fighting. Lawyer's hourly rates range from $200 to $500, or more. In addition to lawyer's fees, the litigation process usually includes the fees of other professionals like accountants, economists, engineers, or psychologists. In addition are other costs of litigation like computer support, exhibit production, and the costs of transcripts.

A few years ago, I was called into a situation of two brothers who were partners in a third-generation family business. They had reached an impasse over the strategic direction the company would take. They believed they had to engage in a battle about placing a value on the business. Each brother hired a lawyer, and each lawyer retained a forensic accountant to place a value on the business. By the time I was called in, they had stopped speaking to each other based on their respective lawyers' advice. In just the preliminary stages of the battle, they had spent over $60,000 on legal fees, and they were just beginning.

Productivity Cost

Time is a valuable, limited commodity. When people are focused on rehashing the past, they cannot create and produce value in the present. There are two aspects of this cost: (1) the cost measured by diminished current productivity, and (2) opportunity cost. The direct cost is the value of a person's time. This is what the person might be earning or producing but is not because he or she is engaged in the conflict and otherwise not productive. The opportunity cost is the value the person might have developed if his or her energy was able to be fully engaged and present, focused on creation and innovation.

Doug and Frank had designed two innovative forms of management "technology." The processes they invented were significant additions to the knowledge base about personal productivity and leadership. They battled for over a year about who owned the intellectual property they had developed. The productivity loss from their feud boggles the mind. Instead of having many students and clients get the value of their discovery, their time was devoted to fighting. The direct loss was their loss in revenue. The opportunity cost consisted of the value of further innovations that might have been developed during the conflict.

Continuity Cost

Continuity costs accrue when existing relationships are changed. They include the cost to replace someone who can no longer be part of the team because of existing conflict. Gary was on a fast-track management development program. He was transferred to manage a branch office of a financial services company. Unfortunately, he could not get along with Brandy, the office manager. Gary objected to the way Brandy completed reports and the way she socialized with coworkers and clients. Even though she had been doing things her way for many successful years, and even though Gary was aware of the power she had in the office and the local community, he was insistent that she follow policy strictly. He would not back off, and they ended up in a nasty battle. Gary's youth forced him to test his power as the boss. Brandy filed an EEOC complaint and the battle raged for three years after Brandy was fired. Gary left the organization because office performance dropped radically after Brandy left; she had been doing the work of two people.

The cost to train her two replacements and get them up to speed was double Brandy's salary. In addition, the lost revenue measured by the decreased profit was over $200,000 per year.

Emotional Cost

Sometimes there are situations you can't let go of: a fight with a spouse, boss, coworker, neighbor, friend, partner, or the person who ran into your car. The emotions of anger, fear, and blame grip you and force a reaction that saps your productive capacity. Instead of going about your business, you are riveted on the injustice done to you and the untoward behavior of the perpetrator. You are consumed with vengeance and a desire to punish the wrongdoer. You expend energy on your anger, in addition to the loss you have already suffered. This energy will never be recovered.

Randy finally received the promotion he was longing for. That was the good news. The bad news was his inability to focus on his job. He was going through a messy child custody battle with his estranged wife. That stirred up all of the anger he was holding about the past relationship. She wanted to mediate the dispute, but Randy was set on winning. Unfortunately, he lost—his job. It was a position that required all of his attention. He missed two important deadlines because his mind was focused on the past.

You can't put a price tag on these emotional losses, but the cost is huge. What might have been a simple process turned into a situation in which the conflicts escalated and the pain, suffering, and scars were magnified.

Why So Expensive?

Our legal system, the vehicle many people think of as the standard way of resolving conflicts, does not foster resolution. This is because *the operative premise is that someone will win.* Our dispute-resolution machinery often fuels the fire of conflict and impedes resolution. Worse, while engaged in the conflict-resolution process, productive activity (what someone's life is really about) is diluted. Courts do not foster resolutions that address the underlying sources of all conflict—breakdowns in relationship. The process is not designed to get people back to an optimal state of productivity.

The current system embodies struggle, control, and a survival-of-the-fittest mentality. It is based on dialectic, right/wrong, either/or patterns that originated in Aristotelian logic. Even though we live in a densely populated, rapidly changing technological world that cries out for systems that foster collaboration, individuals and institutions are tenaciously clinging to old habits.

Because family structures and religious institutions have become so fragmented, we no longer rely on them to provide the education of core values. Many people seek external standards that will tell them what to do. People often have little grounding in collaborative skills because real partnership flows from within the covenantal relationships that community, family, and religious institutions have traditionally demanded and fostered. Many people have no role models and, sadly, in many instances don't know how to treat each other from within a common covenant.

There is a breakdown in the covenants of trust among people who are members of the same community. They point to a lack of communication. People are focusing on themselves. They are concerned about their rights and entitlements without thinking about their responsibilities toward others. This all flows from the win/lose systems and practices that are in place.

Many people are looking for guideposts and rules that will tell them how to treat each other. This requires new practices and new ways of thinking. As you think about the various costs of conflict, imagine how much more you might accomplish if you could harness the resources expended, the money and energy used in the battle of traditional conflict resolution. Imagine using those resources to produce desired outcomes.

The Value of Agreements for Results

Let's look at the upside productivity value of agreements for results. Can you remember the last time you were a member of a high-performance team that produced results that were way beyond expectation? The essential attributes of a high-performance team are a focus on mutually agreed desired outcomes, no tolerance for conflict or chatter that impacts the mission, immediate behavioral feedback, everyone taking 100 percent responsibility, and a feeling of heart connection to the other members of the team. When those ingredients are in place, and everyone is clear on what they are supposed to do, extraordinary results happen.

Results I have seen include dropping of territorial boundaries for the sake of an outcome, adoption of children, retention of prize employees, effective coparenting from divorced parents, ex-spouse partners making millions, divorcing couples embracing, work teams doubling goals, partnerships recommitting and enjoying exponential growth, a family business saved and thriving. The bottom line is that when we can join our energy with others, synchronicity produces extraordinary power and results. Some of these results are quantifiable, and some cannot be quantified. Remember the Mastercard commercial that demonstrates the joy of certain activities, and as you see the joys the narrator says that some things are "priceless," while for everything else there's Mastercard.

Imagine the value of agreements for results, both as prevention and as substitute for our old thinking patterns. Imagine if you could go directly from a breakdown to an agreement for results.

Summary: A primary benefit of agreement is avoiding the huge cost of conflict that is composed of the following:

1. *Direct cost:* Fees of lawyers and other professionals

2. *Productivity cost:* Value of lost time to the organization: today's value is the direct cost and tomorrow's loss is the opportunity cost of what those involved would additionally produce

3. *Continuity cost:* Loss of ongoing relationships, including the community they embody and the cost of educating new people

4. *Emotional cost:* The pain of focusing on and being held hostage by our emotions that results in the inability to focus completely on what is happening in the present moment

On the positive side, the potential benefits are incalculable.

Exercise: Do you have a situation in your life where the lack of a clear agreement is creating conflict? What is the lack of agreement currently costing you? What is the potential for future costs? Now are you willing to take action?

CHAPTER 39

CREATING A CULTURE OF AGREEMENT: MANAGING BY AGREEMENT, THE NEW MBA

● ● ● ● ● ● ●

I dreamed in a dream
I saw a city invincible
To the whole rest of the earth
I dreamed that was
the new city of Friends,
Nothing was greater there
than the quality of robust love,
it led the rest,
It was seen every hour
In the actions of the men of that city,
And in all their looks and words.
—Walt Whitman, *Leaves of Grass*

Whitman's words are appropriate for an organizational environment. In our personal and family life, love is the accepted context. We don't use that term overtly to describe our organizational environments. And yet the energy of love is where real power comes from; it's what drives high-performance teams and creates bonds in pursuit of a mission. We do well to remind ourselves that Max Depree's articulation of covenantal relationship[13] is the source of

Herman Miller's success. *The Wisdom of Teams* contains hundreds of stories about teams falling in love. The Ten Essential Elements of agreements for results are designed to produce the covenants that generate love. At a profound and fundamental level, we cannot resist this phenomenon; it's woven tightly into the fabric of what it means to be human.

Building a culture of agreement inside an organization is not easy to do. This chapter sets out an overview of what needs to be adopted as a practice. If some of the content seems repetitive, please think of it as a review and summary of the ideas already introduced—just expressed in a composite, comprehensive form. As you go through this chapter, think of how you can apply the information to your own personal and work situations.

A Challenging Time for Organizations

The capacity of technology is far greater than most of us need. Regulation is way behind and trying to catch up to the reality of actual practice. This is true with technology, the Internet, patents, biotechnology, finance, utilities, mergers, etc., etc., etc.! Many people are feeling disoriented because our foundation of standards and accepted ways of doing things has crumbled. We have no solid ground to stand on, and it's not going back to the way it was!

Collaboration is one of the keys to high levels of productivity. But *the old rules about forms of collaboration no longer apply. The only rules that exist are the ones you make up for the particular transaction.* That's why it's so important to have a method that will take care of any collaborative transaction, which is every transaction. The new MBA (Managing by Agreement) cuts through to the core of what gets in the way of the highest levels of performance and productivity. It elegantly creates joint vision and quiets the internal voices of dissonance and conflict (chatter) that get in the way of real partnership. Managing by agreement is the path to relationships based on covenant.

The Source of Dissonance and Conflict

Productivity and satisfaction depend on clear hearts and clear agreements. When the heart or the agreement is unclear, conflict and compromised productivity follow. When I think of entering a new business or personal relationship or a conflict resolution process, I think of a continuum:

1. Stress signals real conflict or fear of conflict in a new project, team, or relationship. *This is our individual reaction.*

2. Self-management (of emotion generated by stress) is a precursor to effective negotiation and collaborative dialogue about the real or potential conflict. *This is a skill we need to learn.*

3. Collaborative dialogue to create clarity takes place, resulting in a new agreement that resolves the conflict, or starts the new venture off on solid ground.

The first element is the context in which organizations operate; there is no shortage of potential supply of dissonance and conflict. The second element reflects the traditional ways people manage their reactions to their emotions, such as visualization, time-outs, dealing with it "tomorrow," exercise, nature, yoga, or "heartmath."[14]

The new MBA takes care of Number 3!

The Management Opportunity

The new century seems much different from 1990. Changes include rampant terrorism, the presence or survival of dot.com mania, knowledge workers, the end of the job, downsizing or rightsizing, reengineering, self-managed organizations, flattening, technology, telecommuting, stock options, free agency, "brand me," the learning organization, merger mania, golden parachutes, executive MBAs, employment litigation, project orientation, work as a primary community, reliance on a "work family," and the virtual organization.

These changes have generated significant conflict and dissonance in organizations—and great opportunity. Unfortunately, most managers (like most other people) are conflict-averse: they don't engage (in fact, generally avoid) conflict until it becomes acute. By then, the costs of conflict are staggering: paying professional consultants, lost productivity, opportunity cost, loss of the benefits of continuing relationships, and the emotional cost that eats at the fabric of every organization's spirit.

When managers do engage with conflict, often they deal only with symptoms and not the root causes. They resist getting near the real source of dissonance. To stop the staggering loss of resources, managers would be well served to learn the skills needed to manage by agreement. The organizational benefits that flow from the competence to prevent and deal with conflict are huge. The ability to resolve conflict and form effective working relationships impacts the core of every organizational function: teaming, managing, partnering, customer servicing, producing, innovating, learning, collaborating, and diversity. I believe that the failure proactively to develop competence in dealing with conflict is a form of mismanagement! Conversely, knowing how to develop effective working agreements is a fundamental competence for managing anything.

How MBA Works

Here is a formula for Managing by Agreement (the new MBA):

The power of agreement + the art of resolution = results beyond expectation

Workplaces have become our dominant social institution, the arena in which we create, produce, and provide, not only for each other's material needs but also for each other's social needs within our work families. *In the 21st century, organizations will not only serve their commercial mission, but they will also be a very important vehicle for taking care of human social needs.* Managing by Agreement contains easy-to-use tools that create partnership and shared commitment in all forms of organizational relationships.

Managing by Agreement creates covenantal relationships that are based on shared commitment to ideas, issues, values, goals, and management processes. The covenant is the true source of real teams and is a key ingredient for having a work family that provides a source of the richness and fulfillment we seek. With covenants in place, results beyond expectation follow. When you start a new project, you will have the tools to create a road map that reminds you of your mission and the route to get you there. If you're deep in conflict, MBA provides a seven-step process to resolution.

Because technology enables capacity far beyond human capability, and regulation lags far behind what people are doing, we need processes that allow us to define how we will work together. Managing by Agreement provides a dynamic context that advances change in organizational cultures. Agreements provide the context that promotes collaboration, teaming, learning, change, and continual improvement. The new MBA provides standard practices through which desired changes can be identified, clarified, and implemented. Individuals and groups are legitimized as they learn how to address their unique needs and concerns. The results are empowerment, teamwork, increased productivity, and self-management.

The Art of Agreement

Productivity and collaboration are functions of effective, explicit agreements! Productivity, and all satisfying professional and personal relationships, results from collaborative action. We collaborate with others in language by forming agreements. These agreements are expressed (spoken or written) or implied (assumed). We often have conflict because we did not take the time, or we never learned how, to craft effective, explicit agreements. This is a skill we were never taught, even though it is fundamental and a foundational life skill.

The causes of wasteful, expensive conflicts are implicit, incomplete agreements that do not express a joint vision and do not solidify relationship in the process of crafting the agreement. This often happens because the process of negotiating an agreement is seen as an adversarial process in which you try to win, as compared to a joint visioning process that expresses an inclusive vision of desired outcomes and sets forth a road map to those desired results.

Agreements impact every aspect of organizational life, including:

- Ability to set and reach goals
- Quality of work
- Quality of work relationships
- Strength of teams
- Amount and intensity of conflict
- Level of trust
- Leadership ability

You can learn how to craft elegant agreements using the Ten Essential Elements of Agreement template from Chapter 2. The ten elements can be used by yourself as goal-setting tools. They can be used to foster covenental partnerships with colleagues, bosses, support staff, suppliers, joint venture partners, clients, and any collaborators. The key is articulating joint vision, the way you will produce desired outcomes, standards to evaluate your results, and who you need to reach your objectives. Managing by Agreement is a simple way of planning and implementation that generates a high level of buy-in because it is empowering, inclusive, and highly participatory.

The Ten Elements of Agreement

1. *Intent and specific vision:* The big picture of what you intend to accomplish together must be specified. The first step of any effective collaboration is sharing a big picture of what you are doing together. This provides a framework on which to hang the details. A joint enterprise works best when everyone is working toward the same specific goals. The clearer the detail of desired outcomes, the more likely you will attain them as visualized.

2. *Roles:* The duties, responsibilities, and commitment of everyone must be clearly defined. Everyone necessary to achieve the desired results must be part of the agreement.

3. *Promises/commitments to action:* The agreement contains clear promises so everyone knows who will do what. When commitments to take action are specific, you can determine if the actions are sufficient to obtain the desired results and what actions are missing.

4. *Time and value:* All promises must have specific deadlines for task completion. These are "by whens" (by when will you do this and by when will you do that). In addition, you need to specify the time period that the agreement will be in force.

Value specifies who gets what for what. Is the exchange satisfactory? Is it fair? Does it provide adequate incentive? This must be clearly understood, and everyone must be satisfied, or someone will sabotage the transaction.

5. *Measurements of satisfaction:* The evidence that everyone has achieved his or her objectives must be clear, direct, and measurable so there can be no disagreement. This element is critical because it eliminates conflict about the ultimate question: Did you accomplish what you set out to do?

6. Concern, risks, and fears: Bringing unspoken difficulties to the surface provides the opportunity to anticipate and minimize the disagreements you know will happen during the collaboration. The discussion will deepen the partnership being created or let you know this is not a partnership you want to be part of.

7. Renegotiation/dissolution: No matter how optimistic and clear you are, it will become necessary to renegotiate promises and conditions of satisfaction. Circumstances change, and you must put in place a mechanism to address the new conditions. Being realistic about this at the beginning enables the relationship to evolve and prosper. It is imperative to provide everyone with a way out—an exit strategy anyone can follow with dignity. Anyone who feels imprisoned in a transaction, partnership, or relationship will not make his or her maximum contribution to the enterprise.

8. Consequences: Although you may not want to police the agreement, it is important to agree on reminders for anyone who breaks a promise and to be mindful of the cost of failing to produce desired results.

9. Conflict resolution: Acknowledge that conflicts and disagreements arise as a matter of course as people work together. If you know that and establish the attitude of resolution and a process that leads to a new agreement, resolving conflicts will be easier.

10. Agreement? Everyone is satisfied and ready to take action. Work on the agreement until you are satisfied that you have an agreement or do not have one. Unless and until you are satisfied, do not move into action. You will not have a shared vision toward which to work. Also, ask yourself whether the outcome will be worth it.

The Seven-Step Process of Resolution

Cycle of Resolution

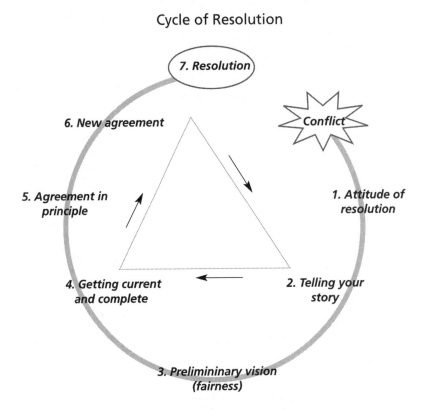

Conflicts, differences, and internal chatter pervade organizational relationships. No matter how good the agreement, conflicts and differences will surface. The ability to prevent destructive conflict (dissonance that gets in the way of productivity) and always move toward resolution and agreement is a critical core competence. Resolution, and a new agreement that articulates the resolution, increases productivity and returns everyone to optimal levels of output and satisfaction.

Resolution restores the ability and desire to take action, coordinate action, and see the productive benefits of our collaboration. *Getting to Resolution* enables effective collaboration by allowing everyone to focus on productive activity, not on the conflict.

The seven-step resolution process includes:

Step 1. *Attitude of resolution:* New thinking about conflict/agreement

Step 2. *Telling your story:* Everyone's uninterrupted turn to speak

Step 3. *Preliminary vision:* The focus on what would be fair to everyone

Step 4. *Getting current and complete:* Letting go and leaving the past behind

Step 5. *Agreement in principle:* What is the new relationship?

Step 6. *New agreement:* Details and plan for the new relationship

Step 7. *Resolution:* In action and productivity, without chatter

Step 1. Developing the Attitude of Resolution

The ten principles of the new paradigm hold the values that make up the Attitude of Resolution. This attitude is the place of beginning, a critical first step This will not develop at once; it will take time to change the way you think. This is the foundational step. The goal is to internalize the principles.

Step 2. Telling Your Story

The second step is telling your story and listening to all others' stories, including yours. It is about understanding and being understood, one of the *Seven Habits of Highly Effective People* that Steven Covey inspires us to cultivate. If you learn to listen with a careful ear and honor everyone's story about a situation, you take a big step toward getting to resolution.

Step 3. Listening for a Preliminary Vision of Resolution

The third step is to start thinking about a resolution that honors all concerns in the situation. It is about shifting from the desire to win (get your way) to a vision that everyone can buy into. It comes from a sense of fairness. This initial vision may change as you gather more information and learn more.

Step 4. Getting Current and Complete

The fourth step demands saying difficult, sometimes gut-wrenching, things. It is about articulating what usually goes unexpressed and escaping from the emotional and intellectual prisons that keep us locked in the past. It is a way to face the good and bad in any situation and to experience and grieve for the disappointment of unrealized expectations. It is a way to put all of the detail out on the table and choose those remnants that can be used to weave a new tapestry of resolution.

Step 5. Seeing a Vision for the Future: Agreement in Principle

Now that you have a preliminary vision, along with the information and emotional freedom provided by the completion process, you are ready for the fifth step—reaching an agreement in principle. Having looked at what other people need and noticing the cracks in your perhaps righteous position, you are ready to reach a general understanding of the resolution. This is the foundation of a new agreement. You let go of the desire for what you know will not work, and you focus on what will.

Step 6. Crafting the New Agreement: Making the Vision into Reality

In the sixth step, you put specifics onto the agreement in principle. You design and construct a detailed vision of the future. You have a map, a formula for the dialogue that will maximize the potential for everyone to obtain their desired results. The more time you spend in detailing the desired results, the greater the chance that you will realize them.

Step 7. Resolution: When Your Agreement Becomes Reality

The seventh and final step is moving back into action. With a new agreement and a quiet, clear mind about the past, you can freely move forward, devoting your energy and intention to currently desired outcomes. You will have a new and profound sense of freedom because you have spoken all the unspeakables. You have completed the past and constructed a clear picture of the future and of the highway that will get you there. You will be empowered by the process. You are resolved.

As you work with resolution, you learn how to recognize conflict patterns, discover and address everyone's real concerns, honor differences, and legitimize all perspectives

The new MBA has an immediate impact on:

Working relationships	Diversity and gender issues
Work group productivity	Creativity and innovation
e-Commerce	Mood and attitude
Vendor relationships	Conflict resolution
Litigation/employee lawsuits	Customer satisfaction

The nature of organizational life will not revert to a state of hierarchy and order.

Managing by Agreement is an effective alternative to chaos. It provides tools that serve, enhance, clarify, and provide a structure within which you can "make it up as you go along" while fully allowing principles of self-organization to operate. I believe that the balance of self-made structure and self-organization can provide the context in which individuals and organizations flourish.

Managing by Agreement produces clarity about where you are going and the route you will take, before you move into action.

Summary: The new MBA cuts through to the core of what gets in the way of the highest levels of performance and productivity. It elegantly creates joint vision and quiets the internal voices of dissonance and conflict (chatter) that get in the way of real partnership. Managing by Agreement is the path to relationships based on covenant.

Exercise: Is there conflict in any organization you are a part of? Does that conflict hamper the mission you are trying to accomplish? Enroll others with you in applying the models of the new MBA to quiet the conflict and prevent it from resurfacing.

CHAPTER 40

DESIGNING AN IMPLEMENTATION PLAN

• • • • • • •

I will view all lands as though they belong to me, and my own as though they
belonged to mankind. I will so live as to remember that I was born for others,
and I will thank nature on this account; for in what fashion could she have done
better for me? She has given me alone to all, and all to me alone. . . .
I will do nothing because of public opinion, but everything because of conscience.

—Seneca

I hope you find Seneca's remarks inspiring. I hope that at this time you have been able to recognize the value of agreements, and that you are motivated to change the world in your immediate vicinity out of a consciousness of conscience because you have come to recognize that it is a better way.

If you like what you just read and find yourself motivated to make changes in your home, family, or organization, there are some key things you need to keep in mind before you start to impact any culture. Exactly how you move forward depends on the context. There is no cookie-cutter right way to start a change process. Only you know the players and the territory you will be navigating. Here are some guiding principles I have found useful.

Guiding Principles

Fear of zealots: My experience is that most people fear zealots who come with "the" answer. Even if you are excited by possibility, please dampen your enthusiasm for the purpose of achieving the impact you want.

Start anywhere: You don't have to be the CEO, executive director, patriarch, or person who has influence. If you believe you have a good idea, you do, and your good idea will attract the resources it needs to grow and flower.

Make a plan: If you don't know where you are going, any road will get you there! Before you whip into action, remember *Ready, Aim, Fire.* Use the agreement model to structure a plan with yourself.

Make a clear case: Remember that the best, most convincing case for a culture of agreement is to be fully aware of the large cost of conflict. Take the time to analyze the cost of conflict in your organization or family. Make conservative assumptions and projections, and you will still see huge transaction costs of the current "organizational" conflict.

Build a team: You can't do this alone. Look around you for people you think will understand what you are saying. Recruit them.

Enroll broad support: To have a successful initiative, you must get people on board from all levels and all departments of the organization. Remember that playing organizational politics is nothing more than jumping into the soup of organizational decision making and making your voice heard. It's not dirty business unless you play it that way.

Manage up: The art of organizational effectiveness requires managing your initiatives in all directions. If you see things you don't like and ways to improve them, make your voice heard. You are not being compensated for holding a place. Initiative and results are the values you bring.

Find a champion: It's not essential, but if you can convince a senior person of the value of your ideas, the road will be easier, doors will open, and you will have resources.

Nothing to lose: The best attitude is not to be attached to any particular outcome for your initiative. Yes, you care. Yes, you present your ideas well. Yes, you move forward with passion. But you are not attached to an outcome. Although you can influence, you cannot control others. If people are not ready for whatever gifts you bring, accept that now is not the time, move on, and devote your energy elsewhere. What you learn in the process will help in your next attempt.

Start with a pilot: No matter how good the idea, everyone in your context will want proof of success. The best way to gather that, with minimal risk, is to begin with a pilot. This will allow you to test the waters, and it will provide useful feedback for modifying your tactics.

Teach and learn, learn and teach: Remember that personal and organizational improvement are about learning new skills. The best way to learn is to teach. Always remember that the process of change is fundamentally an educational process that happens through the vehicle of communication. We receive information from others, and then we communicate with ourselves about what we received. Then we make decisions about the actions we will take.

Stay conscious of your resistance: Remember that the value of the new information will only be realized if you can control your own resistance to change.

Dignity of beginning: The best way to quiet your resistance to change is to embrace the dignity of beginning. When we first start any new activity, we are not competent; we are beginners. Through learning we become competent. If we can accept and talk to ourselves about the process of change as a learning experience (like riding a bicycle, driving a car, or using a computer), we will be able to laugh at our incompetence, stay engaged, and gain the new competence we desire. If we don't do that, we run the danger of running away, because no one likes the feeling of incompetence.

Simple, not easy: Remember, the principles and models expressed in this book are very simple. They are not intellectually challenging. They are not rocket science in terms of cognitive understanding. They are challenging to use and to implement because they are counterintuitive to almost everything you have learned about this area of human interaction. Remember, *Agreements for results represents a huge paradigm shift. It's not easy being on the bleeding edge.* Believe me, I have the scars to prove it!

Don't get pickled: My favorite theory about change is the Pickle Barrel Principle. It says that no matter how hard a cucumber resists, it will turn into a pickle when placed in the pickle barrel. Stay mindful, and look for small victories.

Celebrate success: The best way to reinforce positive results for both an organization and an individual is publicly to celebrate the accomplishment. That will make the individuals proud, and at the beginning of a project it will generate enthusiasm and enroll other "users." Since success breeds success, you will generate the beginning of a movement.

I wish you the best and trust you will reap what you sow. Please sow the fabric of agreement into your cloth and into the fabric of those you contact. You have the skills to do so. The work is now up to you.

> *Those of us who walk in light must help the ones in darkness up*
> *For that's what life is all about, and love is all there is to life.*
> —Anonymous

ENDNOTES

• • • • • • •

1. Levine, Stewart. *Getting to Resolution: Turning Conflict into Collaboration* (San Francisco: Berrett-Koehler, 1998).

2. A client who had a flair for promotion coined this phrase as I guided him through a series of sensitive negotiations.

3. DePree, Max. *Leadership Is an Art* (New York: Doubleday, 1989).

4. DePree, Max. *Leadership Jazz* (New York: Doubleday, 1992).

5. Senge, Peter. *The Fifth Discipline* (New York: Doubleday/ Currency, 1990).

6. For example, see Korten, David, *The Post Corporate World, Life after Capitalism* (San Francisco: Berrett-Koehler, and Hartford: Kumarian Press, 1999).

6a. Ray, Paul, and Sherry Ruth Anderson. *The Cultural Creatives: How 50 Million People Are Changing the World* (New York: Harmony Books, 2000).

7. Svendsen, Ann. *The Stakeholder Strategy* (San Francisco: Berrett-Koehler, 1998).

8. Weisbord, Marvin, and Sandra Janoff. *Future Search: An Action Guide to Finding Common Ground in Organizations and Communities* (San Francisco: Berrett-Koehler, 1995).

9. Peck, M. Scott, *The Road Less Traveled*. (New York: Simon & Schuster, 1978).

10. Neimark, Paul. *Same Time Next Week* (New York: Crown, 1981).

11. For the gift of the idea of Permanent Domains of Concern, I am indebted to Fernando Flores, a consultant and teacher from the San Francisco Bay Area with whom I had the privilege of studying. He is the CEO of Business Design Associates.

12. 2000 Annual Report of the Federal Judicial Center, (www.fjc.gov).

13. DePree, Max. *Leadership Is an Art* (New York: Doubleday, 1989).

14. Childre, Doc, and Howard Martin, with Donna Beech. *The Heartmath Solution* (San Francisco: HarperSanFrancisco, 1999).

SELECTED BIBLIOGRAPHY

● ● ● ● ● ● ●

Avery, Christopher, with Erin O'Toole Murphy and Meri Aaron Walker. *Teamwork is an Individual Skill* (San Francisco: Berrett-Koehler, 2001).

Axelrod, Richard. *Terms of Engagement* (San Francisco: Berrett-Koehler, 2000).

Bell, Chip. *Customers as Partners* (San Francisco: Berrett-Koehler, 1994).

Block, Peter. *The Answer to How Is Yes* (San Francisco: Berrett-Koehler, 2002).

Bush, Robert A., and Joseph P. Folger. *The Promise of Mediation* (San Francisco: Jossey-Bass, 1994).

Chaleff, Ira. *The Courageous Follower* (San Francisco: Berrett-Koehler, 1995).

Childre, Doc, and Bruce Cryer. *From Chaos to Coherence* (Woburn, MA: Butterworth-Heinemann, 1999).

Childre, Doc, and Howard Martin, with Donna Beech. *The Heartmath Solution* (San Francisco: HarperSanFrancisco, 1999).

Coens, Tom, and Mary Jenkins. *Abolishing Performance Appraisals* (San Francisco: Berrett-Koehler, 2000).

Constantino, Cathy, and Christina Merchant. *Designing Conflict Management Systems* (San Francisco: Jossey-Bass, 1996).

Davis, Laura. *I Thought We'd Never Speak* (New York: HarperCollins, 2002).

De Graaf, John, Thomas H. Naylor, and David Wann. *Affluenza* (San Francisco: Berrett-Koehler, 2000).

Dukes, Franklin E., Marina A. Piscolish, and John B. Stephens. *Reaching for Higher Ground in Conflict Resolution* (San Francisco: Jossey-Bass, 2000).

Ewalt, Henry. *Through the Client's Eyes* (Chicago: American Bar Association, 2002).

Farrell, John D., and Richard D. Weaver. *Managers as Facilitators* (San Francisco: Berrett-Koehler, 1997).

Fritz, Robert. *The Path of Least Resistance for Managers* (San Francisco: Berrett-Koehler, 1999).

Goldberg, Marilee C. *The Art of the Question* (New York: Wiley, 1998).

Goleman, Daniel. *Emotional Intelligence* (New York: Bantam, 1995).

Green, Thad B. *Manage to the Individual* (Atlanta: Belief Systems Institute, 1995).

Hall, Stacey, and Jan Brogniez. *Attracting Perfect Customers* (San Francisco: Berrett-Koehler, 2001).

Hateley, B. J. Gallagher, and Warren Schmidt. *Is It Always Right to Be Right?* (New York: Amacom, 2001).

Hawken, Paul. *The Ecology of Commerce* (New York: Harper Business, 1993).

Hertz, Frederick. *Legal Affairs* (New York: Henry Holt, 1998).

Jordan-Evans, Sharon, and Beverly Kaye. *Love 'Em or Lose 'Em* (San Francisco: Berrett-Koehler, 1999).

Kaner, Sam, with Duane Berger, Sara Fisk, Lenny Lind, and Catherine Toldi. *Facilitators' Guide to Participatory Decision Making* (Gabriola Island, British Columbia: New Society, 1996).

Kolb, Deborah, ed. *When Talk Works* (San Francisco: Jossey-Bass, 1994).

Korten, David. *The Post Corporate World* (San Francisco: Berrett-Koehler, 1999).

LaChapelle, David. *Navagating the Tides of Change* (Gabriola Island, British Columbia: New Society, 2001).

Levy, Mark. *Accidental Genius* (San Francisco: Berrett-Koehler, 2000).

Mayer, Bernard. *The Dynamics of Conflict Resolution* (San Francisco: Jossey-Bass, 2000).

Price Waterhouse, LLP. *The Paradox Principles* (Chicago: Irwin, 1996).

Reina, Dennis S., and Michelle Reina. *Trust and Betrayal in the Workplace* (San Francisco: Berrett-Koehler, 1999).

Ruiz, Don Miguel. *The Four Agreements* (San Rafael, CA: Amber-Allen, 1997).

Scott, Gina Graham. *Work with Me* (Palo Alto, CA: Davies Black, 2000).

Simmons, Annette. *The Story Factor* (New York: Perseus, 2001).

Simmons, Annette. *Territorial Games* (New York: Amacom, 1998).

Stoltz, Paul. *Adversity Quotient at Work* (New York: Morrow, 2000).

Svendsen, Ann. *The Stakeholder Strategy* (San Francisco: Berrett-Koehler, 1998).

Weiss, Alan. *Million Dollar Consulting* (New York: McGraw-Hill, 1992).

Wheatley, Margaret. *Turning to One Another* (San Francisco: Wheatley, 2002).

Whyte, David. *The Heart Aroused* (New York: Currency Doubleday, 1994).

INDEX

● ● ● ● ● ● ● ●

ABOUT THE AUTHOR

• • • • • • •

Stewart Levine has been called an "empowerment guru" who creates agreement and resolution in the most difficult circumstances. He is the founder of ResolutionWorks, a consulting and training organization dedicated to providing skills and ways of thinking that people will need to thrive in the next millennium. He spent ten years practicing law before becoming an award-winning marketing executive at AT&T, where he was recognized as a pioneer "intrapreneur." He uses his approach to form teams and joint ventures in a variety of situations. Organizations he has worked for, in the United States and abroad, include American Bar Association, American Express, Chevron, ConAgra, Deloitte & Touche, DC Office of Corporation Counsel, EDS, General Motors, Oracle, IBM, Kaiser, Herman Miller, Hewlett-Packard, Honda, Safeco Insurance, Stanford University, University of San Francisco, and the U.S. Departments of Agriculture and the Navy.

Stewart spent five years as a seminar leader for Career Track and Fred Pryor Seminars. He designed and taught seminars in the United States, Canada, Australia, England, Scotland, Ireland, and New Zealand on a variety of management topics, including leadership, communication, conflict resolution, self-directed teams, advanced customer service, negotiation, dealing with conflict anger and emotion, coaching and counseling skills, project management, persuasive writing, and transition from technical professional to manager.

Stewart Levine has spoken before a variety of audiences, including the American Bar Association, the American Society of Association Executives, the Association of Legal Administrators, the Crossroads Center, the Society for Human Resource Managers, Simon Fraser University Center for Management Innovation,

University of Massachusetts Spirituality in Business Conference, University of San Francisco Executive MBA Alumni Symposium, Society for Professionals in Dispute Resolution, The Esalen Institute, and the Association of Quality Participation.

Stewart is the Chair of the Education Board of the American Bar Association Law Practice Management Section. He was recently featured in an article about trendsetters in the legal profession. His book *Getting to Resolution: Turning Conflict into Collaboration* (Berrett-Koehler 1998) was called a "must-read" by *Law Practice Management* magazine. It was an Executive Book Club Selection; featured by Executive Book Summaries; named one of the 30 Best Business Books of 1998; endorsed by Stephen Covey, author of *Seven Habits of Highly Effective People;* and featured in *The Futurist* magazine. Stewart is an honors graduate of Rutgers Law School, where he was the Student Writing Editor of the Law Review. He served as a Deputy Attorney General for the State of New Jersey and was a Law and Humanities Fellow at Temple Law School, where he was a law teacher. His recent monograph *Managing by Agreement: The New MBA* was selected for inclusion in the 2002 McGraw-Hill *Sourcebook for Team and Organization Development.*

RESOLUTIONWORKS

The mission of ResolutionWorks is creating cultures of agreement and resolution in organizations, government agencies, communities, and families. Most of the content of this book comes from practicing the work every day. If you are intrigued and inspired by what you have read, I can assure you there is more to learn on your road to becoming a Resolutionary, and personal mastery of the material. We deliver the work in the following applications.

KEYNOTES—Inspirational and content rich

FACILITATION—Saving the cost of conflict for organizations, teams, divorces, family, couples, partnerships, executive groups

AGREEMENT/COLLABORATION—Preventing conflict for business partnerships, boards of directors, executive teams, new teams, new relationships

ORGANIZATIONS—Retreat design and facilitation; aligning mission, vision, values, actions; communication skills, management development, creativity and innovation, building learning organizations, team formation, and development

PERSONAL COACHING

LEGAL—Personal counsel and representation; consultant, managing legal experts

www.ResolutionWorks.org

For information on Resolutionary certification, speaking, training, consulting, or other products and services, and to sign up for *The Resolutionary:*

RESOLUTIONWORKS
(301) 657-6240 Washington, DC
(510) 814-1010 San Francisco, CA
(815) 371-1014 Fax
Stewart@ResolutionWorks.com

Berrett-Koehler Publishers

BERRETT-KOEHLER is an independent publisher of books, periodicals, and other publications at the leading edge of new thinking and innovative practice on work, business, management, leadership, stewardship, career development, human resources, entrepreneurship, and global sustainability.

Since the company's founding in 1992, we have been committed to supporting the movement toward a more enlightened world of work by publishing books, periodicals, and other publications that help us to integrate our values with our work and work lives, and to create more humane and effective organizations.

We have chosen to focus on the areas of work, business, and organizations, because these are central elements in many people's lives today. Furthermore, the work world is going through tumultuous changes, from the decline of job security to the rise of new structures for organizing people and work. We believe that change is needed at all levels—individual, organizational, community, and global—and our publications address each of these levels.

We seek to create new lenses for understanding organizations, to legitimize topics that people care deeply about but that current business orthodoxy censors or considers secondary to bottom-line concerns, and to uncover new meaning, means, and ends for our work and work lives.

Please see next pages for other publications from Berrett-Koehler Publishers

Berrett-Koehler Publishers
PO Box 565, Williston, VT 05495-9900
Call toll-free! **800-929-2929** 7 am-9 pm Eastern Standard Time
Or fax your order to 802-864-7627
For fastest service order online: **www.bkconnection.com**